# The Pattern

# THE PATTERN

*An Exploration of Consciousness*

### KEVIN JEFFERS

Los Angeles, CA
2022

THE PATTERN, LLC.
Los Angeles, CA

First Edition 2022
Copyright © 2022 by Kevin Jeffers
Cover Illustration: Kevin Jeffers
Cover Design: Eileen Mao
Book Design: Pablo Capra
All rights reserved

LIBRARY OF CONGRESS CATALOGING-IN-PUBLICATION DATA
Jeffers, Kevin
*The Pattern: An Exploration of Consciousness*
ISBN 979-8-218-03971-4

WEBSITE:
ThePattern.pub
EMAIL:
info@ThePattern.pub

Dedicated to Maxine Jeffers.
From my earliest days in exploring a spiritual life,
Maxine was ever present, guiding me, always vigilant
in seeking knowledge and the expressions of Spirit.

# Contents

**INTRODUCTION** . . . . . . . . . . . . . . . . . . . . . . . . . . . . . 9

**CHAPTER 1: The Journey Home Begins** . . . . . . . . . . . . . . 13
*Failure was the tool Spirit used to move
me to an awareness of its presence.*

**CHAPTER 2: Co-Creating Life** . . . . . . . . . . . . . . . . . . . . . 33
*I am now the same flawed tool, slowly reshaped as a
suitable vehicle of Spirit, used sparingly but lovingly.*

**CHAPTER 3: Transition** . . . . . . . . . . . . . . . . . . . . . . . . . . 41
*Faith is the essential compass of life—
an integral part of Spiritual maturity.*

**CHAPTER 4: Love and Knowledge, Pain and Growth** . . . . 60
*For all of our efforts, it is the expression of love and
degree of knowledge that we gain which shape and
move us in our transition from Spirit to life to Spirit.*

**CHAPTER 5: From the Beginning** . . . . . . . . . . . . . . . . . . 67
*The fruit of personal research—this moving personal
experience—became for me a process of seeing life
as the absolute integration of Spirit, mind, and body.*

**CHAPTER 6: Search for Spirit, New Consciousness** . . . . . 89
*The Pattern seeks balance at every moment, moving
and rippling with changes created by decisions
and actions that our species demands of us.*

**CHAPTER 7: Inherent Resources** . . . . . . . . . . . . . . . . . 101
*The triumph of our integration in Spirit happens
person to person, moment to moment, event to event.*

**CHAPTER 8: Core Essence, Neural Network of Consciousness**.............................. 110
*The Pattern is impregnated with the spark of creation, that essential energy that begins life and ends it.*

**CHAPTER 9: Expressions of the Pattern** ............... 115
*The Pattern is the underpinning design of life itself.*

**CHAPTER 10: Uplift**............................... 131
*In its intricate functioning, the Pattern is an awareness of a gradual, relentless process of change and modification.*

**CHAPTER 11: Personal Transformation** .............. 143
*Transformation is the process of becoming one with the Universal Mind.*

**CHAPTER 12: After Awakening, Balance** ............. 150
*A shift from the old to new consciousness demands our complete attention to who we are in Spirit.*

**CHAPTER 13: Contact**............................ 161
*The ego is not interested in growth, it is only interested in a static position that enhances its power.*

**CHAPTER 14: The Pattern Unfolds Slowly, Life to Life**. . 171
*Spirit knows the results of our efforts: we have all won the game, captured the prize, merged in Spirit, and have left this world forever.*

**CHAPTER 15: The New Consciousness** ............... 190
*We are willing to risk change because we have found the replacement tools that will make the transition from a material-base to a Spiritual-base practical, if not easy.*

**ACKNOWLEDGMENTS**........................ 202

# Introduction

Each of us struggles every day, in increments small and great, responding willingly or not, to the urgings of Spirit to unfold our interior lives. To set the workings of Spirit into motion. We are pushed to change and become, more so by the times we live in, our bodies and minds responding to the vast pressures that push us outwards towards self-realization.

We know on a cellular level that change is occurring. We strive from this level to the next to move outward into greater meaning. A meaning that is personal and unique yet present in all.

Our lives struggle to coalesce into reason and harmony. Deep urgings drive us to reflect and question. Or, if turned inwards, to become frustrated to the point of self-destruction and despair.

Who of us can live for long in unquestioning gratification—without pause or thought? We are not made to remain aware without an interior struggle, to remain focused in the complex overlapping of degrees of consciousness. Life pushes faster to create new life, a form of life that moves towards Spirit, away from self-concern.

*The ever-evolving Pattern shapes our consciousness.*

The Pattern is viewed as linear energetic blue and white lines within a five-dimensional overlying grid, sprinkled with gold like sparks, markers of every life lived. It exists as a fifth-dimension space, flat, elongated, and continuing to stretch throughout our Universe and others. The fifth dimension is particular to our multiple overlapping realities. This grid of the Pattern is endlessly evolving, created of unformed energy not yet expressed by intent into the manifestation of form.

The Pattern exists, existed, will exist as the underlying structure of the development of souls as they are shaped into complex, evolving consciousness. It reshapes as demanded by the needs of each wave of energetic beings as they are created and placed in the cradle of the Earth and passed out into new Universes.

These lines of *uncreated energy* (energy not yet shaped with creative intention into the manifestation of life) support all forms of consciousness. As consciousness is created and birthed into life, it is placed within this Pattern becoming the location for all stages of evolving consciousness.

My first experience of the Pattern was sudden and shocking. I was sitting in my favorite meditation chair, a gray La-Z-Boy recliner, perfectly padded to support my body, relaxing, beginning a slow breath method of slipping into higher consciousness. Suddenly, I felt myself, my soul, lift.

As I shifted consciousness from a body into a subtler state of awareness, my energetic core first became aware of a deep, luminous blackness unrestricted by time or space. Adjusting to this vision, I slowly focused my attention and found myself in a dimensionless field of clear blue and white lines of energy intersecting each other, forming a grid—an energy grid that permeated and embraced all consciousness.

The grid linked all matter, a source of countless manifestations of consciousness. The grid pulsed with individual points of gold light, each point striving for greater self-awareness.

What I experienced that day—what I now call the Pattern— informed the rest of my life, as I strive to know my Soul's origin and destination. Focusing on the Pattern's light allowed me to live a much more subtle spiritual life. Shifting my core energy (what we mean when we say *Soul*) to a more encompassing view of this Pattern, I was able to see and experience the result of the *Creator's intent*: self-consciousness.

# CHAPTER 1:
# THE JOURNEY HOME BEGINS

*Failure was the tool Spirit used to move me
to an awareness of its presence.*

Over the course of my journey to Spirit, I became absolutely certain that the Self animates each of our lives in both the physical world and the spiritual realm. Through the expressions of life, our continuity is expressed by *rebirth*: continuous lives strung one atop another in a rich, intricate sweep that passes through the fire of experience toward the perfection of love and wisdom.

As a child growing up in a small, peaceful town in the Midwest, I filled my hours learning how to plays sports, track small animals, and thrive on bright summer days. At night, as I lay in bed, swirls of multicolored geometric forms rolled and twisted into new shapes until I fell asleep.

Occasionally, small glowing figures would walk through my room, sometimes stopping to look at me. Others ignored me. In church, I was attentive to the Jesus statue whose face seemed to seek out my eyes in sorrow and pain. I had no explanations, no grounding was just a kid imagining these things, but still, even now, I see them again as fresh as the moment I opened my eyes.

How did these multicolored shapes flow so vividly and effortlessly, first coalescing, then moving apart? Who were these silent visitors? There were no answers, so I myself remained silent until I found my grounding in the life of our neighborhood, and these experiences faded into the background, not to be experienced again until years later.

Each of us, chimerical in nature, is a locus of forces where anything can and does happen. Attracting and repelling energy, consciousness shapes every moment—through the intent of our Selves, our inner drive to learn the fullness of love.

Mankind is the *Forever Being*, a timeless, immortal, indestructible creation of Spirit, encompassing a continuousness. Each Soul is enamored. And each of our life stories is the string on existence with which we experience and become witness to a continuous stream of consciousness, from existence to existence, heaven to hell, darkness to light. We are created in Spirit, not in dirt. We are made of dirt and transcend our bodies to merge again into our Higher Selves, the observers, and choreographers of each of our lives.

This Forever Being is enamored with the struggle and strategy of living and survival, and each story it generates—noble or pathetic, heroic or shameful—is ultimately witness to the courage of the Self in its struggle to live a positive, self-fulfilling life.

It seemed to me that life was the inevitable extraordinary struggle for Self-realization. I experienced each life, each identity, suffering, ecstasy, love, hatred, all of the emotions that are part of who we are and why we are here. Mastery to me was balancing the extremes of emotion and thought.

Life is a testament to the strength and commitment of the eternal Self as it progresses through its unique night of darkness into the Light.

The fruits of my own dark night were experienced as I demanded the presence of the Light, the touch of our creators, having gone silent as Spirit waited for this desperate search for Self-meaning. There is no variance from life to life. We are always each of us searching for meaning, through every phase of our personal enlightenment. For me there were moments of clarity within the comforting and loving embrace of Spirit. I strove daily, only to re-experience my failure, a failure to steady my Self within the embracing love of the Light. At the beginning of the journey, this desire, this implacable intent, was not enough to invoke the presence of the Light.

Spirit responds to our intent and waits for us to signal readiness to begin our journey. Around the age of 18, I was writing poetry in the school's cafeteria when I imagined a place of *no space, no air, no energy*. My life seemed to slip into a new level of insight that showed me the discontent I was really feeling—that life had become a barren ground. Creating art, poetry, even life for that matter held no meaning for me.

*What was missing?*

I had friends, enjoyed walking the Chicago city streets. I lived comfortably and kept my own hours. I was healthy, having fun with women, had an active social life, went out on the town, but something was not there.

*What was it?*

I knew then: *man is an island until he rejoins the creative flow of life.*

I wondered how I *could* rejoin the creative flow of life. Like the flash of light, I understood that it was my heritage to merge with Spirit in some future time. And I needed to find that spirit. Now I had nothing there to hold or grasp. Spirit was always just a few steps away from my touch. But I did have the answer to this puzzle—to merge with Spirit required an implacable intent to attract and keep its attention. Like an ally, Spirit would be my guide and teacher.

From this flashing moment, I made it my mission. Year after year, I polished my Spirit until the day Spirit gifted me with its presence.

## 1971–1974 CHICAGO: SPIRITUAL HEALTH READINGS

After high school, I continued my studies in spiritualism and healing. I read many Edgar Cayce books—he gave spiritually sourced "health readings" while in an unconscious state. Cayce was known for going into a seemingly unconscious state, while spiritual advisors and healers spoke through him. This medical channeling was unknown in the United States at that time, and Cayce's experiences opened the door to new thoughts and possibilities in the practice of spiritually sourced medical advice and solutions.

Cayce moved on from medical readings into relating the past lives of himself and others, exploring spirituality, karmic processes, and other topics normally inaccessible to everyday people.

I became focused on the experience of giving an accurate medical and life reading while in a self-induced hypnotic state. Weekly I would go through a process of regression into a deep meditative space of quiet and peace.

I started using a visualization process triggered by a reverse numeric countdown, a standard self-hypnotizing process which induced a deep meditative state. In that moment of perfect stillness, I was able to "see" the body of the person who had asked for a health reading. I "scanned" their body from head to feet, viewing the energy of their body as a grid. I would use the grid to anchor my view from location to location.

Eventually I was able to view, in my head, pictures of their past lives as well as my own. I did not need the help of hypnotic suggestions to regress to that state of knowing. By telling myself to relax and view my body as an energetic composite, I would quickly be able to work with a spiritual guide to speak of a person's medical condition, past lives, and trending future developments. I would always chat with the person who I had just seen from an energetic view and ask them to verify what they

Chapter 1: The Journey Home Begins 17

had experienced. I did not make an effort to be *right* in the reading, using both positive and negative feedback to know what was needed to improve the reading process. Year by year, this form of communicating and working with Spirit improved and created mostly accurate readings for the people who asked for a reading.

In one reading I was given the opportunity to face the ultimate question of my belief in my own services. Someone had recommended my work to a couple seeking health and past-life reading. She was a healer in her own right, and he was a very strong-minded business owner focused on issues of self-realization. Together, they were serious thought leaders who had influenced a large number of people in social adaptation, restructuring beliefs.

Was this accurate work or just active imagination? I would soon have my answer.

I had started using a visualization process by entering a deep meditative state and scanning the physical, emotional, and energetic bodies as presented, reading the colors of various energetic bodies to guide me in the healing process. Each reading was an opportunity to help a person in need. The receiver of the reading sat next to me as I went into the deep meditative state. No contact, no words were exchanged with each person. I preferred no pre-knowledge of their issues/problems. Silence was needed to begin the work of reading their energy bodies.

I believed at the time that the woman wanted a reading to affirm her own experiences. The man was skeptical, there to see "what this was all about." Her reading was thorough—I made suggestions for better health and new approaches to changing her health by enhancing certain chemical reactions that were a result of eating patterns and genetic twists carried forward from her parents.

His goals were different. He carried a very strong, energetic shield, a no-nonsense, "show me" attitude wrapped around strong and acute intelligence. I was accustomed to this attitude—over the years I had met many people like this, cynics or skeptics, people with strong belief cores that did not believe in health scans, also those looking for a gimmick or trick. Or both.

But there were no tricks, no service fees, no darkened room or spiritual presences, no suggestions of benefits for myself. These readings had become my commitment to Spirit, a Spiritual work, free of material considerations and demands. The reading began in the usual manner. Silence, scan, proposed solution. After hearing his wife's reading, the man became curious and attentive, but remained skeptical. I appreciated this. I like skeptics who bring doubt and examination with them. Here was another opportunity to focus and reach for what was needed to be accurate and thorough.

I went into a deep meditative state. The person working with me suggested relaxation and began a backwards count from 100. By the time she reached 98, I was out. A suggestion was made to review the body before me—the receiver—and begin a physical scan then move into any other information that was available.

I did so and seeing his body as nuances of red, blue, purple, and other colors, I saw the status of his body, then looked at his core energy pattern. In this body reading, in a place of No-time, I saw that one leg was shorter than the other and slightly twisted. I noted it and knew when I returned that I would face a decision to speak of this or stay with the scan and other data. Was the foot really shorter and twisted? I had not experienced this sight into structure before. The man walked normally. No limp or twist in his gait, yet now I was about to speak about this finding to someone I had not met before. Well, I thought, *this is what I'm here for.*

After a moment of hesitation, my guide pushed me to speak.

I said, "Your left foot is twisted, the result of a difficult birth, and shorter than the right foot by a few centimeters." That said

I finished the past-life experiences and slowly came back to full waking consciousness. He sat there with a slightly stunned look and proceeded to talk about his leg and his career as a pole-vaulter. The twist had hampered his efforts to dig in with the pole, and the moment of twisting as his body lifted into the air to surmount the horizontal bar was difficult. This had become a significant life disappointment to a well-trained athlete.

I sighed a quiet breath of air. My relationship with my Spiritual guides had again remained true and accurate.

**APRIL 5, 1972: MY JOURNEY HOME BEGINS**

My first journey outside my comfort zone began in my 19$^{th}$ year when I traveled to Greece and the island of Crete. The strong feeling of discontent had driven me to a place where I instantly felt a deep relationship. The symbols and culture of the Minoan people jumped out at me in books and readings. At once, I knew I belonged there. The thirst for touching this place was powerful.

With a few dollars and many aspirations, I spent months rediscovering who I was. One day, while visiting the ancient ruins on the island, I was startled by an uncanny *knowing*—my first vivid connection to a past life. I had been here before, living in the Prince's summer palace, as a bull rider and architect. Prior to this moment, I had "known" places, seeming to visit them in meditations and dreams. This time, however, I was wide awake. I found myself on a long walk searching for the summer palace of the Minoan prince.

As I rested, tired and hungry, I clearly saw an old cart, driven by an old man and a young boy. They were heading up a gravel and stone path and over the hill where I stood. I followed the path, now a paved road, a winding series of S curves. Sure enough, a posted sign for tourists said this road led to the Summer Palace of the Minoan Prince, a residence in the cool hills.

I immediately walked right into an excavation in the back of uncovered walls and foundations. I found a path leading to another sign that said this was the Palace of the Prince. Marble walls, wall paintings, floor covered in watery and geometric fresco designs all flooded into my mind as I stepped into the Queen's room and baths. My trembling fingers touched the marble walls and I saw the images of the people I once knew. My heart was pounding. I feared what they would reveal to me. Every step I took over burnt marble stones, powerful colors of emotion raced through me. I was stepping into *that life.*

Moving with jaunty pride through the deep corridors of this palace I emerged as a bull dancer, free to come and go, a graceful, confident dancer that tumbled in aching beauty over the lethal tips of the bull's horns. Then, without warning, I turned older, my hair grayed, and I knew I had become a designer and engineer, a builder in service of the palace. It was right here where I had lived and loved and died within this fiery womb—a fire set by a loved one in a fit of demented rage, causing the whole Palace to crumble and cave in, falling to the ground.

The impact of re-experiencing that life set the tone of my present life for the years to come. The experience was real, the emotional energy real, and later the Lady of the Palace would visit me. In my kitchen or sitting with family and friends, closed doors would suddenly open and close as if admitting someone.

I carried the marble fragment across Crete, Greece, and Turkey then returned home after experiencing a lucid dream in Turkey, a fishing village named Barton, near the Black Sea. I knew then the prompting of the dream was urgent. "Come home, come home. Your life work begins." There was no bus in that remote village, so I hired an ambulance returning to Istanbul, lying flat for more than 10 hours on a patient stretcher. From that incredibly vibrant city, after visiting the Santa Sophia with a goodbye, I took a train back to Athens, then a flight to Chicago's O'Hare

Airport and home.

Soon after my return, in a small kitchen in Chicago, surrounded by family, My sister introduced me to a spiritual thought leader, psychic, healer and "sensitive." This was a woman who was well known for being an excellent psychometric reader (someone who can touch an object and experience the energetic signature of its previous owner or one who held the object). I gave her a fragment of white, aged marble from a reception room that once showed glorious mosaics of Cretan bull dancers

She held the fragment and seemed to withdraw into herself. The reader looked into my eyes and said the stone had called out to me because I had lived there—but encased in the stone was tragedy... and a love story.

Just as she told me this, I felt a building of a tangible presence. Suddenly, the kitchen's side door swung open, seemingly by a gusting wind, and a moment later the inner screen door opened. There then appeared a swirling, smoky shape that everyone in the room could see. The shape defined itself into a human form and a hand reached out to me, asking for forgiveness.

*Forgiveness for what?*

At once in my mind's eye, I saw a terrible fire, dense black smoke, and could feel myself choking. The fire had been started deep in the rooms of the palace and raged outwards. The fire was started by the broken-minded woman I loved—Persiphae. I ran throughout the palace hallways calling out her name again and again, "Persiphae! Persiphae!" Panicked and driven to find her. Finally, the blanket of dark smoke enveloped me, and there I died.

In this small kitchen room, a vibrating piece of stone became an access channel for a spirit seeking redemption from a loved one. Persiphae had returned to me to ask for forgiveness for that terrible death by smoke and fire.

I was stunned as images and colors filled my mind. Of course, feeling her love after these thousands of years, how could I still hold that bitterness locked in my psyche. I nodded in acceptance, forgiving her, then a wreath of deeply scented purple lavender filled the room as I held the marble stone. I'd found in that far away palace a Gateway to Spirit that vibrated as it came to life. The benediction of release and forgiveness opened my heart, healing some part of who I am. For a week, the lingering lavender smell followed me everywhere I went in the house—until I gently asked her to leave. The fact is, I was young and anxious, if not afraid. Living with a spirit that followed me from room to room, without privacy was nerve wracking. I was very young then.

Re-experiencing past lives seemed to accelerate my Self-awareness. I traveled to key locations, re-experiencing past and future lives, opening the gates of past memories, setting free the pent-up emotions of centuries if not thousands of years of lives, healing the scars of tragedy, abuse, betrayal, sad deaths also reliving the glory of those moments when Spirit touched my Self, when love healed, however temporarily, a wounded heart. Each place, each moment of these experiences completed me, releasing yet another portion of my unconscious being.

## SEPTEMBER 15, 1972:
## LIVES THAT OPEN THE GATES TO OTHER LIVES

From Crete, through northern Greece, the old Macedonia, I traveled to Turkey with new friends into what seemed at that time to be an open world waiting for me. I didn't know yet that I was destined to grasp the subtle presence of Self in the thick layers of my mind and body, a sense of Self as limitless potential, a unique expression and deep yearning for Spiritual completion waiting to be set free. Still, Spirit's location remained shrouded in the dark of Self.

In the quiet of these places I visited and lived, self-reflection and thought is respected, and I became aware of this deep, unyielding yearning. I could see it in the eyes and expressions of the people around me. Yet, they did not seem to touch my *essence*. At the time, I did not know it is in the nature of man to deny Spiritual reality, however enticing. I sought a creative rush that would take over, opening the door to a foreknowing of limitless consciousness. I searched for truth, then moved on, never realizing that the locus where the experience of Self would be realized was *in* myself.

As a 19-year-old full of fire, I could easily have gone on to India as I had planned, to live my life wrapped in mystery. Unknown at that time, that visit was reserved for later years when I was more mature in Spirit. In a small fishing town in southern Turkey near Russia, I had a dream—both vivid and colorful—a dreamscape—in which Spirit called out to me and pulled me back, urging me to return home, back to where I had begun this journey. The call was clear, and I listened carefully. As there were no other distractions, perhaps choice came from a purer space of being. In the face of such power, there seemed little choice. And so I returned to Constantinople, then to Athens, then home to Chicago with a newfound clarity and peace.

This summoning pushed me through the incredible spaces of ignorance and set beliefs, from the "me then" to the "me now." I was pulled in a way that managed to squeeze Self through incredible doubt and disbelief. My fragmented being synthesized into a frame that could somehow complete the journey as an aware being.

I worked to polish my soul so that Spirit would be attracted to my Core Consciousness. I studied the mystery arts: of healing, trances, meditation, manifestations, and evocations. Each became a fresh page in my life as the urge to go on became stronger.

The reasons were simple: Spirit is always available but ineffable. A tap on the shoulder by Spirit is experienced by each of us differently. Spirit tapped me after I had lived through years of review and adjustment. It was only then that I realized Spirit was always there for me. First, I had to struggle through my mental limitations, conceptualizing an energy that was personal and waiting for me to beckon to it with heart and mind.

I was always unable to bring the large concept of God, the Infinite, into my finite and narrow worldview. I misread each moment. I came to realize that what seemed to be the continuous outpouring of emotion and turmoil was really the intricate, balanced redistribution of Spirit's energy in my awareness. The futility of my life was really, in fact, the intense effort of Self to breach the walls of self-imposed limitations. Worries, fears, anxiety, confusion all lifted in the presence of the Light.

The perfection of balance experienced in the House of our Creator became intolerable. My search for Self-freedom demanded a breaking from my Creator. The beginning acts of life in the earth Energy Sphere became Senseless acts of violence on others, and in turn myself. Each achieved separation from my Father's House. Like the chisel that carves beauty from marble and the inspiration that drives uncontrolled passions, every choice was balanced with a consequence. I learned the depth of my Self in the vivid, simple moments and decisions of each moment of life. As I fell from the Grace of perfection into the dark night of my Soul, each moment, whether emotional, creative, or energetic, focused on self-indulgence.

Actions and thought, winning, losing, indifference, each blended together to become the swirling movement of Spiritual energy permeating through my own affairs and the affairs of all men and women. The Creator could be found in an energetic balance, from the uncertainty of faith to the release from the confines of present-day human consciousness.

*It was within this framework that I began to experience the shape and presence of the Pattern.*

*I first experienced the Pattern as a layered construct, undermining the dream of reality—endless layers of sparkling light that linked all forms of consciousness. The Pattern became present when I needed it most—it was a fundamental explanation of where I lived and grew, expanding my consciousness of Spirit from self-indulgence into Spiritual growth. I became more than my wants and needs; I became aware of the possibilities of a higher consciousness that would lift each Soul from the mire we exist in.*

The path to the vision of the Pattern of the new consciousness of man did not come gently. It was thunderous, sad, furious; exciting moments encased in despair and triumph. As I grew in experience, so knowledge and achievement diminished me. Business success grew tiresome. Spiritual readings became a sorrow, as each contact became an opening to the agonies and sorrows of others.

The shell between them and me thickened with time. They were not me; they were of another place. My life and art became an expression of this sorrow. There was never enough time to look outwards. There was never enough compassion to reach out and heal. My mind became filled with knowledge while the Spirit within me became diminished with the seeming grind of living; my life ran down, as did my life's energies. Nothing was enough, nothing would brighten my Spirit again. Life had pulled me through too many hoops. I knew too much, but so very little.

I came to know that the expression of life is forever changing within the Pattern reshaping our view of the developing structure of a new consciousness. Then I saw the Pattern as an overlay of awareness. The available energetic creation of a higher consciousness was the opportunity for true release—out of the strictures of self-belief into participation of the unfolding of our Total Self.

My search for an authentic experience of Spirit—for the origin of my struggle through material existence toward consciousness—began as a search for my own truth. I was a young man, strong, restless, and driven to find answers to limitless possibilities. There was no centering in the moments of Now. Although I traveled to see new sights, new landscapes, new sensations—all vibrating off of distant places in China, Europe, Asia—these did not puncture my conceptions of what was real, and what was not. What I knew then was insufficient. I simply could not merge my desire with the Light. There was a wedge, a split between my "beliefs" and the ethereal reality of Spirit I was experiencing.

And so, I set out to explore my inner visions. The visions outside me were not as powerful as those within me. A temple in India, an ancient learning center in China, monolithic ruins in Europe, cathedrals, temples, works of art, all added to my swiftly expanding reality. The search for Spirit became the work of my life, my grail, an achievement I believed to be worthy of a life's commitment.

I searched for *years*, examining text and beliefs. I read everything I could get my hands on—Castaneda, theosophic writings of Blavatsky, Edgar Cayce, Rudolf Steiner. I traveled the world, visiting and praying in Tibet's most distinguished monasteries and temples, walked in the glory of Rome and India, entering the small ancient places of worship that radiate with the accumulated power of prayer. Piece by piece I experienced past lives, recovering the shattered remnants of that which was I, like recreating a shattered puzzle of Self. Everywhere added to my knowledge of Self.

*A hard truth: none of this was completely satisfying. Much came close, true. But nowhere in the physical plain could I find the full force of the Pattern of our Core Consciousness.*

I turned inward, examining every room and corner of my Self for the truths I might carry within. Finally, after years of struggle and self-examination, after years of sweating out the guilt and darkness of my Soul, unearthing and releasing accumulated fears, sorrows, frustrations, and hatreds, *finally* I found the core of Self, the fundamental energetic reality of the composition of Self. A spinning, shimmering sphere of colors, composed of small, sparkling dots, expanding into a dazzling radiance of white light that did not hurt my eyes. This paradox—and expanding awareness—became a perpetual marker of the reality of Self.

In the judgment room of Self, where no angel walked, where no voice controls, where thought is spun as brilliantly as crystal, Self judges itself in its own harsh, peculiar light. There was *no love* and there was *all love*.

My Higher Self was ruthless, casting a judgment more final than any earthly peer could render or enforce. In that space I learned that each of us judges ourselves in the privacy of our own Self, with the fiery brands of our own verdict. We live each life, sometimes repeating ourselves for hundreds of years, until the energy we create shifts and moves us into the Light where the practical, brilliant presence of Spirit holds no judgment, no condemnation—only acceptance and love.

## 1977: A BROTHER'S HEALING

I was visiting friends in Chicago when I got a distressing call. It was early morning, and my Mother was on the line, and she was very upset. She said my brother, an All-American hockey player, had been in a brutal collision playing hockey in St. Louis, Missouri. It was the final game of his season and college career as he prepared to graduate that year. The accident was bad. She was told his L1 vertebra was shattered; X-rays showed bone was embedded in his spinal cord. He was paralyzed from the waist down.

At the time I received her call, my brother was in a drug-induced, pain-killing cloud, unaware of the extent of his injury.

My Mother told me to be ready to travel. She knew my healing experiences and hoped once again they would successfully call out to Spirit's bidding. Mom hoped that with the intervention of Spirit, its Light would transcend the grievous injury and open an opportunity for healing. How effective this would be she didn't know, couldn't know. And, of course, he was her son, my brother—it was a frightening and painful call.

We left that morning and drove non-stop for six hours to St. Louis. We were in a van crowded with family. During the trip I was sleepy and stretched out in the rear section of the van. Very soon into the drive, I felt myself leave my body and enter into another place I had never been before. I was told I was asleep for almost five hours, not awakening until we reached the hospital at 11 a.m. Internally, I was experiencing the intensity or preparation for a healing process. We all walked to the nurse's station, expecting the worst news.

My Mother met with the doctor and eventually waved me over. On a light box in the hallway, the doctors showed us an X-ray of my brother's spinal column. We learned he would probably never walk again. A 6'2" athlete in the prime of his life, now crippled. I felt my Mom's heart tear apart. My guts were screaming in shared pain. She nodded at me. I knew what I needed to do.

We entered his room and stood at the foot of the hospital bed. He was in a Stryker frame, hanging immobile in the air. I was at first sickened. I knew that this was beyond anything I had ever experienced or done before.

Yet with the certainty of Spirit's presence, I shifted into a deep meditation, feeling the inflow of Spirit into my body, awareness expanding, full of the presence of the Light. I raised my arms in a gesture of supplication and healing. A startling energy passed through my arms and hands. My body seemed to swell to the point of extreme discomfort. Then a white, golden energy leapt out though my hands to where my brother lay. I saw many hands, many presences in the room, each projecting the light of healing.

I lost track of time and place; my consciousness consumed my sense of location. This could have been minutes or hours. At the time, I didn't know. I shared with him later that I saw hands extend out of my own hands, where the pieces of bone were put back together like a puzzle—Spirits hands at work.

My Mom stood outside, and she and my sister persuaded a nurse not to enter. After doing this for almost an hour, the flow ended and, extremely fatigued, I fell backwards into a chair. My Mom and sister came in, saw my sagging posture, and sat down. My Self was wrung out of energy, like water squeezed from a sponge. I was spent, my head reeling, unsteady.

Eventually, half-dazed, I got up out of the chair and walked out, wandering the hospital's hallways. I needed to walk, to regain my strength. I didn't want to go back into that room.

Sometime later, my Mother found me and asked me to talk with the attending physician. Something had changed. The Doctor had walked into the room holding up a new series of X-rays just a few hours after the healing.

He indicated to my Mom and sister that the shattered bone was gone, the pieces had migrated back to the L1 vertebra. They called me to the light box. The Doctor was visibly upset and confused. He had strong words about the X-ray technicians sending the wrong film. The doctor apologized to my Mother for needless emotional pain. I was puzzled and asked him what other spinal injuries he had treated recently, and he said, "None—the film we saw before must have been from another patient." When I pressed him on the matter of whom the film belonged to, he could not say.

Sometime later the next day, my brother's prognosis was upgraded from a life-debilitating injury into one that, given a body cast and a great deal of therapy, might let him walk again. The doctor said that possibly later in life he might need a wheelchair, he simply did not know, and finally conceded that we were in uncharted territory as the change in diagnosis confirmed a change in status. We left the next day and now the hard work was up to my brother. All of us were indeed in uncharted territory.

My brother later asked me what I had done. He knew my past work. I asked him what he saw. He said, "I saw you, and many presences of you, on each side of the bed, hands held out, directing a healing energy of bright light."

He asked how this could be? I told him I didn't know, and I really didn't know. I had prayed for his healing, and it happened. He was happy and stunned with the change of prognosis. In time he regained full feeling in his lower extremities. He could walk again.

We left the next day. A new set of X-rays showed the same image as before, the shattered vertebra had migrated back to the L1. I slept most of trip back, my heart and soul wondering about what had just happened. My brother, much older now, plays golf every weekend, hikes, and bikes frequently, and has walked many soccer fields teaching his two kids the finer points of soccer, a sport he always excelled in. And both of us are still navigating in the uncharted territory of the One, the Maker, the Spirit.

I know now that I sought the healing of peace within myself, the power to express self-realization, finally moving into the glory of the brilliant light of Spirit.

I remember as a six-year-old going into a large church and gazing up at the nailed God hung on a cross in blood and anguish. Looking and finding stillness I asked the lifeless statue to merge with the Core Consciousness that already resided in my heart. I asked and prayed that he be aware of me, protect me, nourish me, be a part of my life. I committed my life to Him, baring my young, innocent soul, inviting this presence into me. The statue seemed to move as its eyes radiated a presence, an acceptance of my commitment. He seemed to say in my mind that He would be with me as I was with Him. That commitment has never diminished in the cycles of my life.

Later, I would know that the Core Consciousness was the collective Self Group of all forms of consciousness within the Earth Energy System. This Core Consciousness, however it chooses to express itself, became my Father and Mother. The science of asking, the dynamics of prayer, the stillness of meditation weren't known to me at that time; I had only one thing going for me: trust—an absolute, irrevocable, undeniable trust. I was born with this and have retained it throughout my life. Core Consciousness was always there, a quiet sure presence that touched me in clear, undeniable ways. There was no doubt, there is no doubt. This became the centering experience in my life. No doubt about it: my Core Consciousness simply *is*.

**EVERY STORY HAS A BEGINNING. THIS IS MINE.**

I was born in a small Georgia town and grew up in an even smaller Ohio town, a village of farms harvesting wheat, corn, and soy. Childhood was spent wandering through lush fields, sometimes tracking small animals, uncovering hidden spaces, and I was filled with joy.

Still, in the vast space I grew up in, there was no preparation for my spiritual search later in life.

Like many, I first knew Self as a concept taught through various religions, schools, and spiritual readings. I grew into a disciplined mind, guided by teachers in life and Spirit, and I willed myself to survive. To survive in the jungle of man, I had to keep the truth front and center.

I collected the tools for witnessing Self, moving to the locus of where the event of Self-realization would occur. First prayer then meditation pushed me out into the spiritual world, as every realization, every experience, allowed me to gain personal power, building my heart and mind into a functioning channel for Spirit to manifest itself. I did not doubt its occurrence; the certainty of awakening within Spirit was written in my heart, inevitable. All that I knew and realized within my Self was really of little comfort. I needed—no, I *demanded* more.

Always, in the background, I felt that something important was missing, a piece left unfinished somewhere inside me, an irritation in my Soul that would fire up my awareness of a greater potential in my self-consciousness. I lived with an energetic wound of fear and doubt. If not attended to, this would grow out of control, leading into the unknown country of my Soul. The persistence of this feeling, the fear of being left behind in some way, the agony of incompletion, goaded me into movement. I simply could not keep still, but each new location only made me want to move again. *I myself* was the itch that could not be scratched.

# CHAPTER 2:
# CO-CREATING LIFE

*I am now the same flawed tool, slowly reshaped as a suitable vehicle of Spirit, used sparingly but lovingly.*

**1987**

The greater part of our total spiritual Self is not directly engaged in the functioning of our daily lives. What we experience here is a partial identity, a segment of a consciousness that exists on multiple levels of reality.

Earth was built so that we and all forms of consciousness can learn to function and thrive within a system of self-survival, gaining the immeasurable wisdom of living in a predatory system of life. The skills and experience we gain from lifetime to lifetime frame the future reality of who we will become as we rejoin our personal Total Self, the full expression of Spirit manifested as light and wisdom.

To enter the earth plane within the package we call consciousness, we are self-programmed to experience life in the needed format to learn and complete our fractured Selves. A fracturing that occurs when we first enter the earth life cycle that we agreed to become a part of as the beginning of our time here. Location, genetic structures, sex preference, intelligence as chosen are all expressions of self-divinity combining to guide the expression of our life.

Spirit chooses moment by moment to push us into experiences that move us towards completion. Nothing happens in our lives that is not a result of our cooperation with our Total Self. Death, illness, incapacitation, encounters with violent outcomes first go through our group soul, guided by counseling and consideration of effects, towards a desired result.

Taken in context we are who we decide to be, live as we choose, encounter life as we allow. Our greater Self exists outside of time and space and knows before we are born the outcome of our lives, all pointing towards Self-realization.

The decisions we make are less spontaneous than judged. Lottery wins, an inheritance, the gift of a loving touch, the support of unknown friends showing up in our space are all calculated to keep us moving forward.

The results of this life, lives past and yet to be experienced, are known in a moment by our total Selves. We are gifted with choice of action and thought, each contributing to the quality and content of our lives. We are greater than we think, our Spirits surviving and thriving, learning and experiencing, to that moment (known) when we will again join our Total Self.

### 1994: ROME, ITALY

In Rome, visiting churches and early Christian tunnels, at the Colosseum where I was fortunate to see the gates below the royal viewing stands, I re-experienced life as a Roman soldier, of royal lineage, caught by the militia for secretly practicing the beliefs of Christianity in the catacombs.

I was sentenced in the Rome Colosseum by the Emperor himself. My sister now and then was caught up as well in the arrests and also faced a death sentence. There was no mercy, our sentence had to be made official, as a practitioner of the Christian followers and prominent in Roman society. I died in that show place, a spectacle for entertainment, as happy and boisterous crowds watched the Christians torn apart by lions. I stood there, a soldier of many battles, a member of royalty in this new Rome, and awaited death. There was no fear: soldiers knew how to accept death. Tightly I held the hand of my little sister, letting her know I was there. She also died with me on that day. Interestingly, in this life, I met that lion and there seemed to be a connection. I was not its meat that day.

## 1996: BEIJING, CHINA

In Beijing, China, I walked the streets of Beihai Park, attracted to the White Dagoba, a Buddhist temple, feeling the pull of Spirit. It was in this quiet park that I passed through an old Tibetan Buddhist sanctuary where each new Chinese emperor was consecrated. Here I found myself and recovered a piece of who I am.

## OTHER TIMES

I fought in the Civil War battle of the Glorietta Pass in New Mexico, receiving a mortal wound, learning in Spirit how to lead the dead to the City of Lights, a skill gained and never forgotten.

I walked through the old streets of London and remembered a life of beggary, shunned by everyone as my body ruptured with leprosy—a slow, miserable death.

## JERUSALEM

In Jerusalem and Acre, during the French Crusades, I lived as a Knight Templar. Warrior and priest, I was captured, and died with my Brothers when, kneeling, a Saracen blade severed my head from my body on the hot, blood-drenched dry sands.

All these past lives were experienced and released as the remaining essence of Self, embraced, and joined within the community of consciousness that formed my Total Self. The stories continued throughout my life up to that time, the reclamation of aspects of Selves coming to an end as, in this life, I reach the ending of my current Self.

Piece by piece, I recovered my past Selves, placing them in my heart. I became stronger in Spirit, strong enough to see past the veil of my physicality. The journeying from place to place was magnificent, yet I always felt some critical piece of data, some essential understanding was missing. I was more than the parts of my being. What that was, what it looked like, would become another life journey, not outward but inward.

I did not yet know what that meant or where it would lead.

### MAASTRICHT, NETHERLANDS

Inside the old city of Maastricht, I visited Oude Minderbroederskerk Chapel, built in 1234 on the site of many other temples and altars dating well before the Roman occupation. I was caught in a memory have having lived here. This chapel vibrated with age and depth, prayer and devotion, so intensely I could reach out and touch it. There in front of that simple stone altar another piece of a life was retrieved.

## Growth and Depth

### 1997: MEXICO CITY, MEXICO

I traveled to Mexico City for business, and then to Tenochtitlán where I saw my past life in the nobility, then my sacrifice to Huitzilopochtli, a deity of war, sun, human sacrifice, and the patron of the city of Tenochtitlán. On the temple steps, the High

Priestess held me and cut out my heart. I knew the priestess who did this, a sister in that life, also in my current family. As royalty, I gave my life willingly to a blood sacrifice as a prayer to the Gods, a price paid for rain in the midst of drought. I died drugged, in religious ecstasy, and I ascended to the Gods. Exhausted, I returned to the hotel and collapsed, but the memories of the day have never left me.

**THE DEATH OF SPIRIT, A TERRIBLE ANGUISH**

At 38, I found myself hovering above my body. Diminished in life, having lost my visions and heavy in heart, I was ready to leave. There was no pull from this life to stay, so I moved out of my tired body into the grayness that diminished my sight, passing through the countless restless souls who could not reach out to the Light. There, among their screams and moans, they sought to hold me back. I met family members, saw the brilliant yellow light, and through the many layers of realities we pass through upon death, to the place from where one does not return. The song of defeat had carried me to my end, and I embraced it.

Sometimes death is inevitable, sometimes it is torn from life, out of turn. My small death was the beginning of my life. I moved as a flow of gray light brightening into white, to that place of entry, a higher life, where I saw the image of a white-robed being guarding the border between here and there. I knew the next step, the next thought would propel me past the Guardian. Uncaring, accepting, I stepped forward. I saw he was holding up his hand, blocking my entry. With a great push the Guardian sent me back, end-over-end, back through the gray spaces into the body that lay on the bed.

Shoved down into my body, into physical reality again, I was forced to live. I had been rejected from freedom by a moment of indecision. The desire to end myself fled as the desire of Spirit made itself clear. *Life. Continuation.* I didn't know then the anguish soon to come, the anguish of restructuring myself. Had I but known, I would have cringed like a broken animal, begging not to go through what I would have to endure.

Spirit, in its relentless love, pushed me away from the freedom of its home and into the now. I found myself back in my heavy, uncooperative body—the uncherished temple of my life.

I didn't give a damn!

Here I was, once again in the hot seat.

It took three years of restructuring my life, my thoughts, my intent, the desires of body and being, before the gift of that rejection would become clear.

In that moment, I was worn and soiled from life, unable to process and reconcile this world with the experiences of the Self.

My conscious Self became a sponge, absorbing every moment, indiscriminate, unable to grasp the Patterns or the meanings of Spirit. I had eaten too well of life. I knew the illusion of being, the heartbreak of intelligence without purpose, of having tasted Spirit and laid it aside for smaller gifts. I did not know the compassion and love of Spirit, its absolute commitment to me, or its ruthless bending of will to achieve its purpose. I was a flawed tool without wisdom or compassion for myself or others.

The following is a poem written at that time, expressing the experience of the Self's willingness to reengage in the experience of Spirit's love.

> Bereft of what man is given as a gift, he walked through the sublime portal of the holy place, remembering a child who spoke the sweet Core Consciousness language of innocence to the ancients embedded within its white marble altars.
>
> Kneeling in unsure genuflection on forest-green rails, each movement a tempest of doubt, his hand crossed then re-crossed the vast barriers separating him from his Core Consciousness, then fell

gracefully into the track of his faith.

Attuned to the winds blowing through his dry Self, no longer driven onward by dead voices, a sweet full voice filled the empty spaces of that twilight holiness, a Selfless praise, a dreaming aching gift of love.

This lucid voice pressed through the discomfort of flesh to Spirit, forming a soft luminescence, an articulated breath of life descending in subdued brilliance through his obtrusive heart, then calmed, he breathed out.

Whispers of haunting clarity intoned by liquid words moved in and through him, "You are blessed," as soft hands touched sweat-drenched brow, effecting a profound change in this place of being.

Accepting that simple phrase echoing within his astonished heart, its clear judgment an aching intensity, forever would he hear again the loud persistent echo of grace, the foretelling of completion.

## THE HARD REALITY OF SPIRITUAL GROWTH

I am now the same flawed tool, slowly reshaped as a suitable vehicle of Spirit, used sparingly but lovingly. Looking back, I see my being in the context of a life with a Spiritual calling.

*The results are true to the beckoning.*

My life in the here and now was created to accomplish the reclamation of my Self's myriad energy aspects, left on earth in previous incarnations of consciousness, all linked to the living energy of Spirit, I moved to this space through the portal of failure—a life characterized by consistently missed opportunity to embrace and align with Spirit. Along the way, I was marred by shortcomings in which I incurred such elementary mistakes that I had to laugh at the bitterness and tears of this dark comedy of Life. Little did I know that we enter our distinct realities blind to our relationship with Spirit.

Persisting in the disarray of failure and sadness, I was driven, if not flogged, onwards by the sweet taste of Spirit's blessing. At an early age, I was certain that Spirit knew of my inconsistencies, my vagaries of intent, my mastery of self-misdirection. I had been touched by its presence despite failure.

A friend once said to me, "Failure is the tool Spirit used to move me to an awareness of its presence." I knew this to be true.

Failure has been the cornerstone on which the success of my quest for self-awareness was built.

Failure acted as the crucible of my Self, forcing me to refine my vision of Spirit, to teach the difference between belief and reality, desire and intent, Spirit and illusion.

Failure was the engine that drove my Self forward, the fire of this quest, the excruciating payment.

My story tells the visions and experiences of one man's re-creation of consciousness, from an inward-flowing focus towards a singularizing of identity, from a continuous flow of fragmented moments of *now* redirected to an outward flow of consciousness, into the eternal presence of Spirit. As the years of my life have passed, I have continued to be drawn to various locations, cities, temples, churches, usually places of worship, yet not always.

My past lives were often mundane, concerned with living and surviving within the cultural mandates of that time. Again and again, I reincarnated to expiate spiritual transgressions, to balance a wrong action, or to simply rest from lives spent in action. In each Life, I left a portion of Self, inevitable when one is born in the Earth Energy System. The spark that joins a sperm into an egg to create a life requires a spark of Self. An energetic outflow that embeds in the womb is then expressed as a life. Birth is a debt which accrues a cost, and that cost is left behind at death. Most of us are not shamans and priests who can pull their life energy with them at death. In the circle of our lives from creation to departure, we must reclaim these abandoned sparks of Self or remain anchored to the earth *as others in our souls.*

# CHAPTER 3:
# TRANSITION

*Faith is the essential compass of life—
an integral part of Spiritual maturity.*

The transition from ordinary reality to the vivid expansion of a separate reality was not casual or without effort. From the time I returned from my wanderings as a young man, I embraced the search for extraordinary reality. My knowledge of Spirit was small. At that age and that time, lasting years, I was anxious to move directly into the First Cause. I had no interest in the mundane; the demands of life were more burden than privilege.

My heart was rich in its desire for Spirit, but poor in experience. There were no building blocks in place, no supra-structure to stand upon. Every moment, every discovery moved as sand through a mesh, lost as it flowed away in the wind of the years.

How could Spirit call me forth and deny me the simplest experience of Self, a reunion with the Creator?

The process of moving within Spirit became a gradual demolition of beliefs, thoughts, and experiences—the elements which welded me to this reality. I didn't know that the base structure of experiencing Spirit was the simplicity in which people approached their Core Consciousness.

It was not through intermediaries that our Selves flowed into the moment of now, the blending of consciousness into a single flame of knowing. Struggle was as necessary as passion. Spirit does not listen to our explanations; it is attracted by the passion of Self and its purity of energy, purity that is heated and tempered in the fires of Spiritual consciousness.

This I saw was the foundation of extraordinary reality. We were not pulled in through Spirit by determination or sweat. Rather, we are seduced into giving our passion and energy directly to Spirit, invited to dance on ephemeral wings, upon the winds of light that encompass the Greater Being. We are beckoned to become one with Spirit within its nurturing light.

*The growth of being comes not from learning, but from the simplicity and passion of being in love with Spirit. Drop the intelligence, strip away the emotions and the pull of earth, lift up your heart, and open your essential Self to the light of Spirit. You will be uplifted by the breath of Core Consciousness into the illumination of being. Look up into the glow of the sun and you will move into the light with grace and wisdom, a gifting of being to the eternal being of Core Consciousness.*

Such extraordinary moments are the visions of the Spirit world, when the mind steps aside, allowing us to become enraptured in the blessing of Core Consciousness's fire.

Spiritual intelligence, faith, is much more than an article of belief, a catechism of dogma. Faith is the essential movement of consciousness through childhood into maturity. It is the movement from self-centering outwards into the expanding universe of self-awareness, and the individualized placement of reality in Spirit. Faith in a supernatural reality coexists with physical reality.

*Faith is the essential compass of life—an integral part of Spiritual maturity.*

Yet, there is no proof—not by word, not by image, and not by personal experience. Each man is his own tempter, his own killing field, a player in the pervasive trend toward man's inhumanity to man. Our systems of ethics and morality, shot through with exceptions and failures, are the violent proof that, as a people, we refuse to pay for the fruits of self-consciousness. Even worse, we are a people so scarred by deep apathy and despair of mind that any effort to assert Spirit as a functioning core of personal reality becomes predetermined to fail.

Every road to Spiritual fulfillment lies cloaked in symbols and mystery. Our religions are draped in the invincibility of doctrine, and our science is embedded in a pragmatism that excludes the subtleties of mind and heart.

Man's Spiritual world, his most personal description of an interior experience, is rendered useless in the face of a greater consensus agreement. Each of us is so focused on survival that our most basic energies are directed towards sustaining life and deriving what pleasures we can from it.

Meanwhile, the Spiritual experience for each of us is subjected to the dampening influence of habits and beliefs. Our exceptions and variations are scrutinized and tested by the measurements of teachers and mentors. Our words of faith are diminished, and our declarations are stamped void. We measure and test ourselves to the same verifying systems—the Spiritual experience is placed in the realm of the unattainable.

I often pose the question: "Does Core Consciousness have a hand in the affairs of man? Does it have a hand in my own affairs?"

Once, meditating on this question, I experienced a vision that opened the doors of my mind to the workings of Spirit in my life—a direct and immediate transition from *belief* to *experience*.

This vision became a moving personal experience, a direct experience of life as the complete integration of Spirit, mind, and body, a self-sustaining ecosystem that is nourished and driven by a Spiritual source, finding manifestation and completion through physical reality.

My experience of Spirit as a reality came at the moment when my awareness linked with my total Self, the unencumbered Self. I no longer saw life as the consensus agreement that I had to constantly verify and validate physical reality. Instead, I saw life as the result of a *directed force issuing from a Spiritual "thought"*... the primal cause we acknowledge as Core Consciousness.

The directed force was like a blueprint. It required committed workers to implement and complete its evolving design. In this respect, it was like all first-run ideas. The Project Manager's interpreters were an organizing intelligence, issuing directives to their co-workers, the Angelic hierarchy. And like all blueprints or creative templates, it was designed to operate in material form through the expression of energy, regulated by our actions and choices.

As my attention turned inward, seeking again the touch of Spirit, I prayed for *knowing*—simple, blessed knowing. My heart, burnt in the turmoil of life, sought the healing touch of Spirit's love, "Please, move me deeper into the sublime reality of Spirit, for a moment, so that I may experience the deep peace of knowing, embracing movement and presence. Please, Spirit, touch this Self, pull me forward into the depth of your being."

The light within my mind blossomed. I saw before my mind's eye the slow, majestic, revolving earth in a shimmering transparency of multicolored lights. The earth as seen from outside, from a distance that moved all parts into a single being, a revolving orbit of brilliant blues, deep emerald greens, and yellows.

Looking into this picture, I fell forward into it. I saw soft radiating lines that formed a grid around the globe, feeding the vast movement of light beneath its nurturing canopy. All creatures breathed the subtle nourishing light in and out, breathing as one, pulling from this light the essence of life.

We were all there, dancing to this subtle rhythm of light, touching, crossing each other, blending into then separating from each other, leaving, and taking a portion of this mystery as the day moved on.

*The Light of Spirit touches each of us.*

There was no hidden corner of being, no consciousness left unnourished. Occasionally, a brilliant flash of light would erupt. I saw this as people touching the matrix of the grid with their being—a merging of intent with will. Prayer set in motion the upward spiral of light. Each prayer sparked against the light's presence.

The image created *understanding*. We are all nurtured; we all return the light to its source. No one is left untouched. We blend with this light and move ourselves into it. Like breath, we move into the light and retreat with each exhalation.

We are, each of us, each I, present with the light that nourishes us.

We are, each of us, each I, an expression of that light, seeking always to move into its life-giving aura.

We are, each of us, each I, a part of a Pattern that touches our being, through the flesh, into our energy of Self.

*We are because the Light is.*

## 1998: CHANNELING THROUGH AN INTERMEDIARY

Sometimes people are present in the moment of "Now," seeing clearly backwards through time and forwards into the shape and pattern of their and other's lives. These people are unanchored in time and space and operate within an environment where the interface between "here" and "there" is balanced in the needs of each reality.

These very special people use gifts of Spirit in each moment, to far see, heal body and mind, and sometimes tweak the path of someone who stands on the edge of the moment of Now and needs assistance.

This story is about one of these gifted souls, whom I met in my travels. Nothing in my frame of reference would guide me in dealing with and energetically interacting with a living baby Buddha.

### APRIL 1, 1998: A TEMPLE VISIT

In the mountains of Tibet, China, driving to the city of Shigatse, I met the black-robed Baby Buddha (a tulka of accepted lineage). Arriving and entering the visitor parking area I saw many priests cloaked in a black garment with a red interior liner. This was not like the visit to the Potala, where monks were dressed in yellow and orange garments.

I was directed to a building with long lines of people, and bought a white silk scarf to be blessed when I met the baby Buddha. Inside there were many skylights framing rays of light that created in me a deepening shift of consciousness. Eventually the line shortened, and I stood before the seated baby Buddha. I didn't know what to do but had observed others kneeling and bowing. I just knelt eye to eye with the Baby Buddha.

He looked into my eyes and spoke to me, and I had no idea what he was saying. I just knelt and investigated his energy field that radiated streamers of yellow-gold energy. He seemed so young to me, yet he was probably somewhere between 40 and 50 years old.

Finishing his chat he looked intently at me, blessed me with palms touching, bowed, and touched my forehead. I fell backwards, propelled by some energy. His light finger touch sent a shock surging through my head. I remembered getting up as he smiled at me. It was hard to regain my feet. Later a friend confirmed that I had really seemed to be knocked backwards with the touch of his finger, rendered unconscious. When I recovered, the Baby Buddha spoke to me again. I felt dazed and somehow blessed. A completion had occurred, a sense of wholeness.

When I walked away, a young assistant to the Buddha asked me what the Baby Buddha had said—he told my friend the Baby Buddha did not speak to visitors. And I was the sole white face in that room. Why? I had no idea though the priest's request seemed urgent. Why did he speak to me he insisted? I told him that I didn't understand the words. My friend told the priest he was not speaking Chinese, maybe Tibetan.

When I left, I felt somehow whole again. Stepping out into the light of the day, everything carried a brightness and clarity so intense that it should have burned my eyes, but it didn't. I had headaches for months where his finger had lightly touched me.

To be available to the healing process requires a clarification of your intent to heal. Stepping up to the receiver and raising hands or thinking, "Today is a great day for a healing," or other vague beseeching of healing powers to be present, will at its best create a happy glow the receiver.

Creating a specific intent and pushing that intent outward will create a focused stream of energy, usually felt in the hands and arms as heat, a discernible vibration that courses through palms and fingers and seems to leap out to the receiver.

Stating intent, feeling the response of your intent through definitive physical reactions, leads to the most critical aspect of a healing: entrusting yourself to Spirit's presence and direction. This is a very focused intention of the healing process, creating a location for Spirit to move its healing energy to a specific person, a specific location, a specific known illness. Imagining a glow or aura of healing light serves no purpose.

Moving from complete attention to self-generated distractions will break the linkage to Spirit. An effective healing comes from work and focus! The healer needs to be fully present in mind and heart to call on Spirit to heal. Wanting a good result is not enough.

## JUNE 1, 1998: HEALING WITH INTENTION

*Megan's healing*

I was asked by a staff member if I could heal her uterine cancer. She had plans to be married and was afraid this would not happen. A very traditional Catholic, she believed that Spirit would act through me. I was doubtful and I had no certainty this was possible. Cancer?

With personal reservations I accepted her request to work to heal her, or at a minimum slow down the activity of the cancer cells.

On a Saturday morning she came to my house. I said I would proceed but advised her there was no certainty for a positive result. I would go through the process and immerse myself in Spirit. I asked her to lie down and create a receptive mind and heart. She did so, clearly nervous but accepting of what might happen. Hoping for a good result.

I stood and prayed that Spirit would guide me and support her, channeling energy to create a healing event. As is sometimes the case I felt a rush of very warm energy running up my body to my chest. Intention, I reminded myself, and focused as clearly as possible on her energy field. I wasn't sure where to begin so I just began. I used a silver pendulum to attune my awareness to her body and the pendulum moved back and forth. At the area of her abdomen the pendulum began to move from a swing to a very strong circular motion. Here was the location. Now to release the very uncomfortable build up of heat in my hands. The surge of energy was strong. I continued to ask my Guides for help.

I removed myself from the process, stepping aside for the healing work of Spirit. My hands became very hot. The silver chain seemed to burn them. Regardless, I kept my focus and continued. All of this was good. The flow continued for about 10 very uncomfortable minutes then just stopped, rocking me backwards from the disconnect. The pendulum regained a strong swing, indicating the affected area was now working as it should be.

I thanked my guides and stepped away. The process was about 15 minutes. As usual I was slightly disoriented. The presence of Spirit was strong and then gradually dissipated. I asked her to stay where she was and stepped out of the room, collecting myself to talk to her.

I said, "Megan, I have done the best I can, the healing energy was very strong today. When you are ready come to the living room." I didn't have much too say after that, I felt a bit tired, and she seemed to understand. I suggested she thank Spirit and embrace the healing as a gift, which for me was also true.

A week later, the Doctor said she was cancer free, a spontaneous healing. I congratulated her. She would continue to be a bright star in this life.

*There is no explanation for living, no defense for destruction, no justification for being. We are. We live. We are part of the source of life, part of this master template of being, the Pattern that moves within each particle of our being.*

I may call this master template, this creative blueprint of consciousness, *The Pattern*, but in fact it has no name or identity. It is simply Spiritual reality unfolding itself, moment by moment. It is a moving, elegant, flexible art form fed by the intent of the Creator, the master intelligence of life. The Pattern is the organizing principle and management system that allows energy to realize form, allows the creative idea to gain substance and reality—Spiritual reality *and* physical reality, the outward man, and the inner Spirit. This Pattern is the complete management of our Self's evolution from infancy to adulthood. It is the path of its return to the creative spark from which each of us sprang, complete yet unfinished.

The Pattern is the dance of a single life through the complexity of infinite lives, each alone, each grieving from a shared Spiritual death. Cut off from our own Creator, we are forced by our higher Self to stand alone, to stand up to the fierce intensity of life, of having a body, of humanness.

We begin with varying degrees of awareness of the fundamental drive to reunite with our lost Creator. Yet, we quickly lose our self-awareness in the driving pulse and demands of life, like babes dropped in the dark forest of survival.

We are unfamiliar with the true essence of the free will that shapes our reality.

We are neither completely alone nor isolated. Nor are we dependent on wit, nor strength, nor speed.

## 2005: FIRST TIBET EXPERIENCE

*Lhasa and adjoining area*

I visited the Potala in Lhasa, Tibet, and prayed for my soul, hearing the chanting monks hidden in clouds of sweet and sour smelling smoke. And then I journeyed up into the mountains of Tibet and the foothills of Nepal, looking for recovered aspects of Self in temples and monasteries. Monk, Lama, shepherd, temple cleaner, life upon life opened my consciousness to the harmony and serenity of this place. I traveled so many paths that, each time I returned, I remembered my lives, like a flower opening petal by petal. The days of mad wandering were finished. I was complete.

I slipped into the consciousness of myself, an old monk who wandered in time, in place, seeing the presence of the Pattern in all lives, crawling from the mud into an upright humanoid, gazing at from the sparkle of stars to the illuminating brilliance of consciousness. There was a Pattern of consciousness. Each epoch added to the work of the previous flow of consciousness into the next expression of Self.

In that place I looked forward in time, into the luminous Black state of Now, a place of no future and no past. There I found and balanced the needs and wants of future selves that would lead to the merging of all lives into a completed Total Self. In this illuminated state the old monk set the direction of the new expressions of consciousness.

A fundamental shift from intellect was needed going forward. What was love? There was indeed an experienced cosmic love, the distant touch of the Creator's Light. Yes, all paths were known. Yet there was no integration of the jewels offered to me. The purest expression of Love was missing. Balance was needed. So, shaping my future Self, I used the energy of the Pattern to redirect myself to the fullest expression of Love, merging mind and heart into perfected Being.

I had lived many times since that moment, and here I was revisiting the origins of my current life experience. Now I knew I would merge into the future of Self through the experience of and creativity of Love, wrapped within the embrace of mind, guided by my Total Self.

There I sat merged in the presence of Spirit, remembering backwards all that the holy place had meant to me. Within the halls of the Dalai Lama in Lhasa, Tibet, I was free to wander among those religious wonders of the Palace. For some reason, I had known and now knew the meaning and locations of scrolls and books. The impulse to touch these remembrances was very strong.

With joy I collected yet another shattered remnant of a previous life.

**TASHILHUNPO MONASTERY, SHIGATSE, TIBET**

I then visited Tashilhunpo Monastery where I paid an attendant to enter the prayer hall, the rooms of the Panchen Lama. The rooms were filled with rows of prayer benches with chairs, and a tall, elevated platform with golden fabrics, accented in rich red thread on gold cloth. Walls of books and manuscripts filled the room. Toys of the child Panchen Lama were strewn on the floor as though the youngest resident had suddenly left. It was there that I experienced a peace I had not previously thought possible, the visceral thrill of *knowing, without knowing, the source of all because I was all.*

## BUDDHIST TEMPLE IN SHIJIAZHUANG, CHINA

Years later I traveled to Shijiazhuang, China and found—seemingly by accident—the Longxing Temple, settled behind mountains, unsee-able to the naked eye. And yet I was able to give directions to my hosts as their car passed the highway exit! I myself was stunned to suddenly be looking at the Guanyin statue on the north side of Móní-diàn, captivated by its beauty, and I was sure the Guanyin who I have prayed to for years, saw me. In the central temple grounds, the courtyard was empty except for tourists. The vision shifted and I clearly saw a group of young men robed in red, listening to a teacher, clothed in yellow and red. I understood that *I* was that teacher speaking to the smiling listeners, who were looking up into my eyes—and then the scene faded.

Later that night as I lay in bed, sweating and restless in the heat that drifted through an open window, a vast, golden Buddha appeared before me. Unspeaking, he radiated love and acceptance, emotions I could not embrace within my understanding at that time. He was so close, I could have reached out and embraced his presence, but I was unable to do so. Peace entered as He looked at me and spoke a blessing.

## 2006: AACHEN, GERMANY—REVISITING THE GRAIL

In Aachen, Germany, I visited the Aachen Cathedral to see the Roman Catholic Diocese of Aachen. One of the oldest cathedrals in Europe, it was constructed by order of Emperor Charlemagne. I wandered through the rooms, chapels, and meeting rooms past the public altar to another altar of marble and stone, lined with gold candelabras. What brought me to this place of grief and blood?

This is what I saw that day.

In the past life, I was a member of the Knights Templar. The Templars were committed to finding the Grail and its reputed treasures. Using maps, it was decided the treasure of the Grail might be found in Jerusalem. With a crew of Templar brothers, we sailed from Paris, France, where the headquarters of the Templars was based at that time. In the ruins of Herod's temple, we found the Grail alongside many treasures in the subterranean caverns. The heavy lifting of rocks and rubble was hard work. Soldiers turned into laborers, sweating through ferocious heat. No one questioned the hard work.

It took a year just to puncture through rock and rubble. After many false signals we found the treasure: tarnished gold candelabras, coins, and other interesting artifacts. In great secrecy we sailed with the treasure back to France to the Templar headquarters in Paris, where we hid it all again. This hidden treasure became the foundation of the order.

I had been a hidden Knight of the Templars who still held significant land holdings and financial resources. I had come to the attention of the city's ranking Bishop, a sensitive man in his own right, who was certain I knew the location of the Grail and the Templars' treasures. Knowing the death sentence was to be issued, knowing the days of examination and torture to follow, I had placed the Grail into an aligned reality to be retrieved by another.

I was arrested, tortured, and eventually murdered by the church clergy's armed guards, on order of the Bishop who demanded I give them the Grail, ever convinced that I had it. I refused; my vows held strong. After days of torture, the Bishop's soldiers stopped the examination. The Bishop nodded to a guard and soon a double-bladed axe split my head into pieces in a small side room of the church, but I felt nothing, having already commended my soul to Spirit's care.

The Grail has since been found by another who walked the lines of reality. The Grail now resides in an undisclosed location. The experience of touching the Grail completed me in some fashion—another piece from another life, put back into place.

In this Pattern, I experienced the phenomenon of a directive body of Spiritual intelligence that expresses total commitment to our Self's awareness and growth.

This extraordinary intelligence sees us as children set on the path of self-awareness, of Spiritual maturity. It is an intelligence that embraces each of us and all of us. Its arms are open to those who seek reunion, and its patience is steady with those who seek solitude or isolation. It is a perfection of being that encompasses all of life's awareness as benign. Just as children in their inexperience need teachers to solve adult riddles and to master the sophistication of prayer, this encompassing intelligence uses its own agents to facilitate our growth. They are agents in the truest sense, representatives in the court of arbitration, overseeing our evolution, as masters of our immediate futures, friends in our search for reunion.

In this Pattern, I saw the sure, loving touch of a greater intelligence, of light forms radiating a guiding wisdom that touched us in the most intimate portions of our being. They were present in all facets of life, each responsible for a portion of our reality, from the greatest to the least intense spectrum of life. They moved in perfect rhythm, a flow of music and light that most did not see or understand. These majestic forces of light, whose auras spread forth from point to point, enrich us, creating a true synergy of elegance and love.

In that space, I was enraptured with life, profoundly moved to the awareness that, in the lowest moment, when the forces of darkness descended into my heart, I was not alone. I remembered a vision from years before when I had been touched by Spirit, and Spirit whispered into my ear from the soft flowing lines of light that clothed its being: *"You are blessed."* The words echoed in brilliant flashes for months, now dimmed into mere remembrance. And I was blessed—so blessed to have seen life in its fundamental shape.

In the brilliance of this light, I saw, from a universal point of view, flashing hues, archangels, angels, and seraphim, all having experiences from beginning to end, simultaneously in reality. Each was a messenger for Spirit.

From having seen the entire movie of our lives, these entities know where their support and input is of value and when it isn't. They are the guardian angels, the comforters, the workers in the field, and in due course, the parents of our Spiritual identity.

*Spirit's love is ruthless.*

It doesn't care for our discomforts and griefs, as we in turn learn of compassion and love. They do not interfere, relieve us, or let us bypass an experience, regardless of how violent or damaging. They accept our misery and love as the flow of energy through the being of Self that man has used to express consciousness since creation.

The Spirit's workers see us as eternal, immortal players in the field of life. They know the end game. They have seen us all as having already won the battle to self-realization, having gained the fruits of Spiritual growth, since they grasp that it is inevitable. They know us as their peers and friends, as children now struggling to understand, struggling to apply the lessons we so bitterly learn and strive so eagerly to avoid learning.

These workers in the Spiritual field, these managers of the Pattern, are all expressions of the First Cause's creative directive. They adhere to the template of the Pattern with unbending ferocity. Yet, they give us real succor and comfort when we bow our stiff necks and pray. As we ask, so shall we receive—and the Law of Grace is extended to us by a most compassionate Core Consciousness.

I saw that we are managed down to the simplest details, in lives planned to bear specific types of emotional, physical, mental, and Spiritual fruit. We are all designed to endure our special blend of love and misery from conception. It is at that moment that, with their help, we select the vehicle of expression that will be ours as we go forward into life. They know our Spiritual attainment was assured from the beginning of our creation. Yet, we each climb Jacob's Ladder—every rung of it must be stepped upon, every grip taken with care and certainty for support and balance, or surely, we will fall to the ground again.

Unbelievably, it is our job to live *life without error*. Yet, in failure or accomplishment, we must come back again and again, until finally each of us experiences the magnitude of our part in the Great Plan, the upliftment of man as a group to Spiritual attainment. Not one of us is free until all of us are free. Like it or not, and eventually we will like it. We are our brother's keeper. It's as simple as that. The achievement of perfection cannot be accomplished without our weakest brother. There are no perfected masters hidden in the folds of heaven, disdainful of man now that enlightenment has been achieved. There are no saints unheedful of a cry for help, a plea for restraint, or a sigh of relief.

In the years of shifting through my consciousness from the inward to the outward, into the accelerating rings of higher consciousness, I experienced that each of us is responsible for every unkind thought, every small violence, every condemnation incurred through our action or inaction. We stand as our own jury, and our self-sentence is much harsher than that of Spirit's. We are responsible for the thought that sparked our actions; a debt of energy accrued that needs to be repaid in full. Greater violence and injustices incur greater debts. We are indebted through the perfect exchange of energy that moves our ultimate reality forward. Compassion, kindness, and self-sacrifice, small or great, cancel or diminish the accrued debt of our load.

Without doubt, I now shifted my view, seeing this world as a focus point of cause and effect, subject to the nightmares and joys of a perfected cosmic bookkeeping. There is no relief from spiritual debt, positive and negative, until all are paid in full. Our account is balanced.

I saw the physical evidence stacking up neatly beside the Spiritual evidence. Neither belief nor disbelief, acceptance nor contention changes either. We are here for the duration of our agreed upon experience, chained in misery or joy. We are forced with the evolution of our consciousness from one aspect to another, a long roller-coaster ride that moves with abandon and speed through the treacherous curves and hills as our car makes a heart-stopping ascent from darkness to light. It does not matter how long the ride takes until we get it right for all of us. There's no escape, only the perfection of an imperfect consciousness.

The magnitude of this experience at that time could only be filtered through my own understanding of the beliefs and cultural standards from birth through my early 40s. These symbols of reality looked much like a computerized color representation of our planet from space. If I got it wrong, or incomplete, or right in part, there was still nothing I can do until greater understanding rose to the surface. You will fill in the missing pieces, for your indwelling Spirit is profound and as wise as my own. You know of this reality, for you pass through its portal every time you pass into extended consciousness by meditation, prayer, and death.

Everything with this perfect movement of essentials suggests we are all individualized energy Patterns. Each of us is a personalized expression of the Creative Mind, unique in our composition, form, goals, and abilities. As Spiritual entities we constantly experience a broader network of individual- and group-energy Patterns working and living in harmony to the creative directive of greater Spiritual intelligences. We live on the frontiers of Spiritual experience, in earthly expressions of consciousness, sending our life experience home to our Higher self and advisory councils.

I laughed to myself thinking of each of us managing life on the planet and coming up very short of a paradise. As physical beings we simply don't yet have the tools needed to manage the life ecosystem, let alone the balancing act of Spiritual interrelationships we encounter within the Pattern every day. I saw that no entity could grasp the reins of our free-shifting reality. Managers of corporations, governments, religions, and institutions were all simply incapable of effectively managing the lives of their own people.

So, if that's the case, who is looking out for our interests in all of this? Who is making the best decisions for our movements through being, keeping the finger off our personal nuclear button?

We are human, deeply flawed—surely, all can see that most elemental component of humanity? We are flesh, driven by the urgings of self-perpetuation and self-gratification. We are sophisticated biotech machines with childlike urges.

And yet, what is astonishing is that we *are where we are* as a result of the strategic placement of our beings by the Pattern's managers. Within a vast network of related energy structures and substructures, each of us will affect the growth of the whole, through our personal decisions to interact and move in a specific direction.

We may come to view ourselves as the mysteries we really are, but only if we step away from the view that we are "just people, living and dying, as all others." We say that what occurs between these two events is anyone's guess. If belief and proof were to release us for a moment, if justifications and guilt were to fly away, we could see the true being—a flow of miraculous energy—a Spiritual being in a Spiritual body, capable of creation and of a rare love—neither identified by color nor sexed by chromosome.

Our bodies are the vehicle of our consciousness, carefully selected in each life. As Spiritual beings, we are greater than our immediate tragedies and misfortunes. We are magical because in our true identity, there is no death of Self. We are immortals in Spirit. Our fleeting miseries and joys move us closer to our Spiritual goals. We are a part of a greater network of Beings, closely managed in this reality so that our movements and decisions push us in a direction that enriches the collective expression of the Pattern.

Fortunately, we are managed by a greater good, not a lesser evil. We choose each moment to express ourselves, assuming and often achieving clarity in the end result.

The Pattern is the vehicle by which the Creative Mind expresses its intent of self-awareness through the experience of its various component parts. This divine desire affects our destinies, our life Pattern, in this life and all others. It enforces the notion that our fate is inevitable, foreordained, conforming to the requirements of the Pattern.

Yet, as with all paradoxes, the predictability of our personalities and the limitless capability of our Spiritual natures create a turning point in our lifetimes, when they rest in balance. Ultimately, that spells a change in our personal and group destinies.

What was true a moment ago, shall be true again.

# Chapter 4:
# Love and Knowledge,
# Pain and Growth

*For all of our efforts, it is the expression of love and degree of knowledge that we gain which shape and move us in our transition from Spirit to life to Spirit.*

The Pattern is my personal description of a vast Spiritual master plan that transcends beliefs of Core Consciousness. The Creator uplifts man's simplified consciousness to co-creator of reality. I say *beliefs*, as my contact with religions has been institution-based. The notion of a living body of work seems limited to the Spiritualist movement. Most people are enrolled in the concept of accepting a religious form. They worship within the form of the body, instead of the freedom of linking oneself to Spirit in the moment of now, free of form or body.

I know that form is important to the security of worship, but stop, if you will, at the idea of Core Consciousness as a sexed being, a kindly or harsh despot. Picture an invisible Pattern. That Pattern is a place where the responsibility of personal and Spiritual growth lies on each of our willing shoulders. I take sole responsibility for its content and its expression in my life—there are no angels dictating script, no channeling of Spirits.

I have been gifted with a vision of reality that, through time, could be corroborated either in science or holy, mystical script.

From firsthand experience, I believe that we can become free of belief, as soon as we accept a Spiritual directive, a hands-on management system. Being free from belief allows us to become engaged in the real-time experience of Spirit in action. We become our brother's keeper in faith and reality. The battle of our Self doesn't occur somewhere between Core Consciousness and Satan, but within our own minds and hearts.

Each of us struggles to gain preeminence in our fight to gain self-realization. The struggle occurs within the timeless vastness of every waking moment of our lives, both the exciting moments and the boring ones, all between the space of our ears and ultimately in our hearts, through the generosity and compassion we pass along, our hard-earned gifts to others.

Our Selves are the battleground upon which the struggle of self-realization occurs. At times we lose, at times we win. There is no condemnation from Spirit, from the kindly, uninvolved Father. We are quite able to judge ourselves with the power of a larger Self that sees us clearly in the context of an evolving being that has already achieved its liberation.

We are limitless beings capable of extraordinary moments. Our lives may be boring or lifeless. This is not the fault of Spirit, or its issue with us. Spirit is more focused on adjusting our reality so that we maximize an attribute or an attitude. The focus is realizing a portion of being so that the whole Self becomes harmonized with Spirit.

Our daily life may be dreadful. Yet, life taken as a series of lessons becomes incrementally easier to live. The notion that we are given only what we can bear has its corollary in a ruthlessly compassionate being interested in our evolution, not particularly interested in the actual accomplishments or failures of each life.

## 2017: ENERGETIC ATTACHMENTS BY SEPARATE CONSCIOUSNESS, POSSESSION

In my healing work I rarely encounter true spirit possession of a person. There are many mental conditions that describe experiences of an invasive, possessive spirit. Often the sense of possession is the result of an energetic structure attached to a person's energy body.

These attachments are common for all people, ranging from mental and emotional blocks, to linkages made by people for various reasons, to a malevolent intent by someone capable of creating, directing, placing a specific thought/energy form in a targeted attack.

More often the sense of possession, malevolent presence is triggered by anxiety, sometimes by the negative thoughts of someone wishing/focusing an ill-intent for something negative to happen (which are energetic structures and forms—thought forms) embedded in our energy field.

Sometimes these energetic attachments are basic forms of evolving consciousness that need the body's energy to "feed" off the hosts emotions through the victim's nervous system. These attachments are not unusual and may be common in highly charged emotional relationships or situations when etherical forms of consciousness attempt to dominant and control others for their own needs.

Rarely, very rarely is their actual possession. The ability for a discarnate energy to move through the higher frequency of life after death to the dense energy of the earth is almost impossible. The possessing entity looks through many bodies to find an energetic compatibility. It may take years, many lifetimes, to find a perfect match. Once the entity finds a body, it has no interest in letting go.

In 2017 I was asked to deal with this situation. The request being, "Stop this, I am getting out of control." I could see energetically a person existing within the same space of a higher vibrational entity, which was seeking control and an energy feed as it grew in consciousness and presence.

## JUNE 5, 2017:
## REMOVAL OF AN ATTACHED CONSCIOUSNESS

A family friend stopped by my house with his wife and young son. He looked haggard, restless, red eyed from lack of sleep. Edgy. She told me her husband was experiencing dramatic shifts of emotional energy feeling, was slowly losing emotional balance, and not sleeping well. I asked him if he wanted me to find out what was digging into his head and shifting his moods to extremes.

A scan of his energy field showed a presence that had attached itself to him at the back of his head and was drilling its tentacles downward though the spine and nervous system. Fortunately, this process had just started. An entrenched consciousness is very hard to dislodge.

I accepted their request and saw the texture and space of the room shift from a light, airy feeling to a darkening energy. I knew enough to be cautious now. Physical manifestation of dark energy is a prelude to dealing with some form of energetic influence, or some level of possession.

Time to get to work. I asked him to have a seat, then asked his wife to remove their child from the house. I suggested the backyard or the comfort of their car. They quickly left, she threw glances back to me, eyes determined, trusting me to find a cause and solution. She was sensitive enough to understand the work would begin, and that I needed to be alone with her husband. I could not risk their child.

He nodded to me and accepted my presence inside of his

space. The process was simple. I identified a bright ball of orange and red energy spinning around his body.

Rotational kinetic energy is the energy associated with spinning around on an axis. It's an energy of motion, just like linear kinetic energy. A diablo—whirling dervishes of what looked like a spinning column of smoke. Navajo Native Americans believe dust devils are the evil left behind by the dead. To come into contact with one will bring great misfortune. Dust devils are to be feared and respected as evil spirits.

I was surprised when the head of a small, bearded face formed outside of the energy trail and looked at me. Unexpectedly I stepped in and reached out with my pendulum, focusing energy, forming the intent to evict the entity. The dust devil continued to look at me, then popped back into its trailing energy. The presence of a warmth in the pendulum and chain confirmed the work was already in process.

I moved both hands to either side of his head. This would be push and pull as the entity fought to be dislodged. I spoke to it, confirming I did not represent danger to it, I wanted it to leave the body in peace and find its way into the Light. It was not interested in peace and light. It wanted to be fed.

I refuse to attack or destroy invasive consciousnesses. They are here sharing this space with us, mostly unseen. They are some form of consciousness, self-aware, evolving. I prefer to redirect their presence and attention away from their target using the energy of a Spiritual Light to push them out and away. The option of returning to the source of Light is always there for them to take.

The dust devil finally quit fighting and popped out of the man's body. It began to spin around my feet, seeking entry into my energetic field. I laughed. He got a good grade for effort. Finding no toehold in me or the now emotionally wrought man, he left the room, but the darkness, though softening, still remained.

*The sun returned. The soft light filtering through the curtains returned. I talked to the couple and warned them the dust devil would attempt to reenter the man's body. It had spent over 20 Earth years looking for the best host for its growth. Later she told me the dust devil seemed to follow them home but could not pass through the energy screens they built. This would go on for a month until it quit and left them.*

For each of us there is only the recurrence of effort and toil, until finally we die; or so it seems. I see the effort and toil as practice to master our needed skills before moving on to the next effort and toil. There is no end to the evolution of Self. How perfect is perfect? We are composites of energy, an agglomerated energy source continually self-designed to expand and accommodate new energy.

For all of our efforts, it is the expression of love and degree of knowledge that we gain which shapes and moves us in our transition from Spirit to life to Spirit. Spirit is the only aspect of our life experience that stays with us. Emotions, beliefs, circumstances all plague us in the fixed realities we create there, but they do not diminish us. Our expression of love expands us, often saving us from the delusion of life in the afterlife.

Without our Self's ability to continually align itself to the Pattern (which it does oblivious to mind and emotion) we would be unable to create the powerful harmony of the Pattern, the master template in our Spiritual lives. Instead, we would be forced to rely on the finite, limiting experience of mind. Without the organizing and re-energizing principle of the Pattern, we would truly become dysfunctional.

I see the description of the Pattern as an important learning tool for myself and my extended family because it presents an integrated detail of life that is anchored in a Spiritual reality.

I *could* merely be impressed with its beauty, functionality, and power, but no!

There are no exact answers—the Pattern certainly doesn't care to explain itself. It is busy enough mapping the levels of our reality in order to nurture our growth. The idea of demanding answers and getting them is fanciful. Instead, we're forced to look deeper into our personal reality to see for ourselves that we are very involved in the Spiritual world, but mostly choose to ignore it.

The Pattern awakened me to its Spiritual reality simply because my being was attuned to it. I liked the results. It now teaches me how to get from here to there without branding and scarring my mind with beliefs or guilts designed to torture me into Spiritual submission.

## THE PATTERN IS THE EXPLANATION OF THE WORD AS THE CREATOR OF MAN

The Spiritual Word is the ultimate harmony, an expression of energy as the woven, complete symphony of sound whose parts make up the final integrity of a masterpiece. The Pattern is the harmonic framework upon which life expresses itself. It is the path of the Word through our reality.

The Pattern is simply a newer description of an older phenomena of integrated systems working in common purpose to lift us from self-denial—*untruth*—into the realm of self-realization—*truth*. Once you comprehend this system, personal redemption and salvation can be viewed as an aspect of the Pattern, or the Word as Spirit, the outcome of man's individual pursuit in search of unity with Core Consciousness.

To this end, I see the Pattern not as a function of belief, but as a reflection of personal experience, interpreted in the context of a directed, multifaceted Spiritual intelligence active in the affairs of man.

# Chapter 5:
# From the Beginning

*The fruit of personal research—this moving personal experience—became for me a process of seeing life as the absolute integration of Spirit, mind, and body.*

### AUGUST 28, 2021: GAIA

Earth core is the center of the planet earth and is a metallic quartz rock. It is also the location of Mother earth, known as Gaia. This is a newer experience for me, the density of the core moves energy about in odd ways. And it is not black, but a solid, luminescent black that is rather beautiful in design. It is from here that Gaia directs the evolution of all creatures in and on the earth. I do not know how this works, just that it does.

The Gathering is not a location, it is a state of consciousness. My frequency was oscillating before my consciousness shifted to the earth core.

After arrival I walked around the black chamber and saw a priest/king who was not happy to see me. Greetings were a large frown and piercing eyes through a large, full beard. He was on what looked like a throne. To his left sat a woman, also shrouded in gold.

On seeing her I dropped to the floor, face down, and said, "Mother of All." She looked at me, but I couldn't focus. She was simultaneously changing faces, while she looked left and right at the same time, tall, slender, regal. I wasn't sure she was there at all though she felt alive. The General was speaking on her behalf to various groups and individuals who were pleading a case, asking for something, maybe just complaining.

When I stood up and looked at her once again, the General nodded at me as though in agreement with something, possibly approval. I have learned not to ignore or demean Gods and Goddesses. Not healthy. Then I left and returned to The Gathering, very puzzled. So many mysteries in a moment of eternity.

I stepped into the healing device and watched the golden energy scans run though my energetic body. The machine began to remove left over particles of myself, attached to me from the disassembly of my energetic body as I went through a black hole. I lay back and relaxed, this was more of a general cleaning up process, lengthy and tedious, as the healing machine worked to find a center of being from the scattered parts. Unlike the Atlantean experience all of the parts and pieces remained. A long, long process.

For many years and many restless nights, I have spent time thinking and meditating about the apparent inconsistencies I have encountered when comparing holy script (and its description of Core Consciousness in the lives of men) and the seeming randomness of deceit and violence, the sheer brutality, both open and covert, that we witness each day of our lives. In graphic detail, the evidence argues for an empirical world—a world of ruthless cause and effect, fully absent of Core Consciousness in the affairs of man.

I know from my own experience that faith was an integral part of Spiritual maturity. Yet the pervasiveness of man's inhumanity to man—always within the context of "civilizing influences" and "workable ethical systems"—suggests a planet uninterested in the fruits of self-consciousness. At its worst, it seems we live on a planet that reflects a sense of total apathy and despair—twin ills that defeat the application of any method or strategy needed to make the Spirit a functioning aspect of our shared reality.

It seemed as if we were all heirs of Darwin's survival theory *and nothing more*. The road to Spiritual attainment lay cloaked in mysterious symbols. I believed our revered leaders to be empiricists and rationalists, invested in the need to explain and render hard proof for all phenomena, everything subject to science and the measuring stick. Man's word, his *self-proof*, was always to be considered suspect, with every description of the interior experience dismissed as useless or inconsequential.

Often, the Spiritual experience was subjected to the same tests of measurement by our society—our word was not valid, or not valid enough. Our declarations of faith were declared null and void because we subjected ourselves to the same verifying systems that facilitate scientific consensus. Outside of our churches and temples, words of Core Consciousness and faith were always to be considered suspicious. Their proclaimers were looked upon askance, even forced to live in isolation, or with rules imposed to silence or controlled content.

I suffered the ennui that comes with having an inquisitive mind. I'm always encouraged by the environment to snuff out unorthodox thought. I adeptly sidestepped the intricate system of landmines designed to silence an unanswerable form of Spiritual inquisitiveness. If the answer did not fit the approved questions, silence was the answer.

I often ruminated over the same question—*"Does Core Consciousness have a direct hand in the affairs of man, or at least in my own?"* So often, in fact, that it came as a total surprise to me one night that I experienced a shocking realization—the one that has since blossomed into this book.

The fruit of internal research had morphed into a process of seeing life as the absolute integration of Spirit, mind, and body—a complete ecosystem driven by a Spiritual source, finding manifestation and completion through physical reality.

I saw life as the result of a directed force issuing from a Spiritual thought, the primal cause we acknowledge as Core Consciousness.

*That directed thought, like all first-run ideas, was a blueprint that required project managers and workers to achieve completion.*

The project managers—or, as I saw them, angelic entities—were the interpreters, the organizing force who issued directives to their workers. The blueprint was a single creative template designed in material form through the actions and choices of an unknowing mankind.

The experience came at the moment my awareness became linked with my total self—my unencumbered Spiritual self. I saw life not as the consensus universe we constantly verify and validate through physical evidence to assure ourselves of a continuous reality-based life. Rather, I saw the phenomenon of a directive body of Spiritual intelligences that exists and expresses total commitment to the support of our Self's growth to individual awareness.

*From a universal point of view, these archangels, angels, and seraphim see us and our experiences from beginning to end—all simultaneously. Having seen the entire movie of our lives, they know where and when their support and input is of value, and where and when it is not. They are the guardian angels, the daily comforters, the workers in the Spiritual field, and in due course, they are the parents of our Spiritual identity.*

As a group, they are oblivious to our ego's manipulation, our personality's reality management, and the pleadings or acceptance of our daily lives. Their love is ruthless, for they care not one whit for our discomfort as we learn their lessons of compassion and love in turn. They do not interfere, relieve, or let us bypass a needed experience, regardless of how violent or damaging. They see us as eternal, as having already won the battle to self-realization, as having already gained the fruits of Spiritual growth. They know us as their peers. They see us now struggling to understand, struggling to apply the lessons we so bitterly learned. These workers in the Spiritual field—these managers of the Pattern—are all expressions of the First Cause's creative directive. They adhere to the template of the Pattern with unbending ferocity yet give us tangible comfort when we bow our stiff necks and pray for succor.

I saw that we are managed down to the simplest details in lives planned to bear specific types of emotional, physical, mental, and Spiritual fruit. Our Spiritual attainment was assured from the beginning. Yet to climb a ladder, every rung must be stepped upon, every grip taken for support and balance, or surely, we will fall to the ground again. It is our job to live life right. In failure or accomplishment, we come back again and again, until *finally* each of us sees the magnitude of our own job—the uplifting of mankind as a whole to Spiritual attainment. Not one of us is free until all are free—like it or not—and eventually we will all see the extent to which we really are our brother's keepers.

It's as simple as that.

## SEPTEMBER 11, 2021: AN ENERGETIC EXPERIENCE

I met a friend for lunch at the local Thai restaurant. I had been picking up a signal from her that it was time to meet and chat. She is an acupuncturist for the family. When I sat down, the energy started to build around me. I did not pay much attention to this; we have had many discussions on healing and manipulation of energy. Her daughter stopped by for some noodles. She is a sensitive, and watched the energy build, then left when the space became uncomfortable to her.

The space we occupied filled with energy like a moving white cloud around my body. This built up and it seemed to being pour into my energetic body. The last time this had happened was a spiritual healing of a friend who had been diagnosed with an aggressive cancer. For some reason Spirit intervened and healed her.

Now my energy body from the waist up started to rhythmically rock back and forth. I could feel the movement from one side to the other. Like an inverted pendulum the rocking was smooth but strong. The pressure to be conscious was starting to be overbearing. I felt my consciousness start to close down.

I became very annoyed at this closing down, without my consent, of consciousness, and knew at the same time that to stay present I needed to push the energy out as it demanded. I held out my left hand and she knew this technique of energy bridging from previous experiences when some similar exchanges like this had happened, though never this strong. I felt sad. For Spirit to manifest like this, she was probably very sick. Or facing danger.

She placed her right hand on top of my left and I placed my right hand above her proffered hand. There was instant discharge of the accumulated energy, like an electric spark of two live wires, arching outwards. The energy drained from myself and the space around my body. She jumped backwards.

It took a few moments to regain my sense of balance, then I sat back and sipped a glass of tea. When I sensed the atmosphere around us had settled down, I asked her what her experience was. She said a jolt of energy coursed through her, then almost pushed her etheric body out of her physical body. Interesting. I explained my own experience of rocking.

I could see through her energetic body. Streaks of color swirled clockwise in the center of her chest. This was not a healing. Spirit stepped in to strengthen her etheric body and add power/strength to her healing work. Seeing this I felt much better and soon left to return home.

I joked with her about her new powers, and though she did not see the humor, it was impossible to ignore what had just happened.

We gain strength and direction as we see in detail the subtleties of Spiritual energies, their ordered placement in our lives, as well as the actual, active intervention of the Creative Mind in our daily lives. There is no force greater than that of the Spirit, for gradually everyone is converted to its power.

With contact, the opening of the channel in our internal receivers—the mystery of prayer—comes full circle: we request, and our requests are considered. We return to the fruit of our faith. Our unflinching knowledge that we will be heard gives us an internal strength, unhindered by the events of life that inevitably weaken our resolve.

The view that the world is fashioned and enforced by strength, fear, and domination is a child's dream, evolved from the years of helplessness enforced by parents and teachers. Strength has no reality over people who are unwilling to be victims. No government can ultimately succeed in its effort to control. They are denied control through the active, invasive effect of Spirit. We are not meant or destined to be eternally manipulated and controlled by force.

When we hear and clearly see the impulse of Spirit, we break the chains of personal bondage to the consensus reality. It is only a wonder that the power structures that control our lives are not more active in their intervention of unorthodox, inventive, and creative minds.

Every unkind thought, every small violence or condemnation incurred through our action and the thought that sparked it, accrues *a debt of energy* that will need to be repaid in full. Greater violence and injustices incur greater debts. We live in a world of cause and effect, subject to the nightmare of its rigid balance.

The scientists in the context of physical reality are right. There is no relief until all debts are paid. I saw the physical evidence stacking up neatly beside the Spiritual evidence; neither belief nor contention will change either. We are here for the duration, however long that takes. Or as I saw it, as long as it takes to get it right, for all of us.

As individuals we are related by common experience. Yet, we are only where we are through the strategic placement of our beings by the Pattern's managers. We are where we are within a vast network of related energy structures and substructures.

Each of us will affect the growth of the whole through our decisions to interact and move in a specific direction. From the higher planes of consciousness that we leave behind at birth, within this timeless point of consciousness, a decision or a choice has little meaning on our location within the timelessness of supra-consciousness. We are self-driven creators, structuring our life's environment, relatives, family, workplace, or physical comforts.

But if we stand aside from the precious view that we are mere people who live and die—and if we acknowledge that what occurs between these two events is anyone's guess—we begin to view ourselves as *energy* or Spiritual beings, neither identified by color nor sexed by chromosomes. We are the vehicle, the body of our choice—a choice we have forgotten for the moment. As Spiritual beings we are greater than our tragedies and misfortunes. We are, in a sense, magical because, in our true Spiritual identity, there is no death, only fleeting miseries that each move us closer to our ultimate goal. We begin to see ourselves as part of a greater network of managed beings. We are managed such that our movements and decisions push us all in a direction that suits the guidelines of the Pattern and the goals of its managers.

The Pattern is the vehicle by which the Creative Mind expresses its intent of self-awareness through the experience of its component parts. This divine desire affects our destinies—our life Pattern. This life, and all others, is foreordained, and conforms to the requirements of the Pattern. Yet, as in all paradoxes, there is the predictability of our personalities juxtaposed with the limitless capability of our Spiritual natures. Within each of us is a turning point in our lifetimes. It rests in balance, a moment of change in direction, a change in the quality of how we express energy, and ultimately, how we fulfill our personal and group destinies.

Most of our lives are lived as an abstraction within our mind, tied to our perceptions, unresolved guilts, and anguishes. We live cloaked in apparently terminal flesh that brings periodic joys and sudden pains. We are neither fully real to ourselves nor our loved ones. Occasionally, we do become aware that our decisions have definite impact in reality, an implacable result in our lives that cannot be altered, once committed. We then grieve.

We are aware from firsthand experience that throughout our lives—lives that appear to be mostly futile and unchangeable—an opportunity to turn the whole mess around may arise as a result of the merest whiff of circumstance or chance. We set new directions that imply greatness in its course—a super-reality of potential. We miss the passing tide, drifting once again into the endless loop of self-condemnation, or else we take ourselves out into the vaster experience of the oceans.

This is the essence of growth from the Spirit's view.

We take risks to break out of old, unusable, or stale, though comfortable, Patterns into new ones that we haven't mastered yet. The risks are the catalyst for growth—the beginning of personal maturation. Mistakes that occur in the process of taking the risks toward Self-growth aren't condemned or judged; they are simply evaluated for results and effectiveness.

Using the master template created to guide the process of personal Spiritual growth, we stand as our own judge and jury: we compare the result of our actions and ultimately pass judgment upon ourselves from a Spiritual point of view. Our self-accounting is complete and final. As we bobble reality for the sake of gain, greed, or acquisition, we absolutely pay the price in kind. The Pattern demands balance from our Spirits, and ultimately, we agree. Our human minds defer payment until it is absolutely necessary, that is our nature, but we grasp the inevitable.

With each of man's futile efforts to move forward as a group, we learn more: nothing is wasted, nothing is empty. Each appropriate motion, decision, and effort accrues the precious energy needed to build self-awareness to the point of self-mastery. All is vanity and futility. It is only through Self-maturity that we are strong enough to continue the vast task of growing up into our responsibilities as self-aware humans.

We are not in it for satisfaction with small accomplishments, but for entry into a bigger picture. As we accumulate more energy through effort and risk, we move in a more focused direction towards the mastery and not the control of relationships, all within the ecosphere of ultimate life—the Pattern. As a group we are facing childhood's end; old, useless Patterns are unceremoniously booted out to make way for new vibrant ones.

The conclusion of my experience—my vision of the Pattern—was that I was gaining insight into a master template which coexisted on all levels of reality, from source or Spirit to its eventual manifestation as physical reality. The Pattern isn't a new concept developed to explain life. It is an old description of The Creator's hand in the affairs of man, except The Creator is not the distant father, but a living Spiritual being acting in unison with a creative force to guide and help us towards the goals of self-mastery.

We are ultimately the co-creators of reality, and the interim apprentices of our own creation.

There are references to life's template, the Spiritual Pattern, in the holy script of every age and culture. It is seen in the New Age explorations of today. Each agrees that life is a manifestation of Spirit directed by our own Core Consciousness, following Patterns of expression that conform to the highest ideals of that age of man. The difference I saw in these interpretations was the active though benign influence of Spirit beings, guardian angels, and Spirits. They act in concert with a directed plan through all levels of man's reality. The end purpose is to lift us up in our evolutionary process from new creations of Spirit to co-creators of the Spiritual order.

The Pattern is our own *personal* Pattern—of self-awareness, changing for each of us as we move forward to the point where we realize ourselves as a part of a whole. As interconnected bodies of energy—part of a harmonious landscape—we are not the isolated point that we spend our lives protecting and ultimately dying for. Isolation from the community is a function of ego that strives to gain power over its environment to assure its continued survival. We are not ego, thoughts, or emotions. We are the limitless expression of Spirit, capable of infinite growth potential.

*Given our inclination to rest—our natural ascension to entropy—we would fall into ourselves in rhythm to the collapsing impulse of the universe if we were without the binding template of the Pattern.* The Pattern acts as a rubber band, stretching until it too returns to its natural shape. Without our Self's ability to continually reference itself to the Pattern, which it does oblivious to mind and emotion, we would be unable to create its powerful harmony—the master template of our Spiritual lives. Instead, we would be forced to rely on the finite, limiting experience of mind.

Why did I have this particular experience? I really don't know! I might have preferred my personal belief system—that if I worked hard enough, kept a modicum of integrity in my personal dealings, and didn't screw business associates, I'd grow into a contented adulthood, with enough money and personal satisfaction to feel darn good about myself until the day I die.

In fact, I do not believe I am particularly suited to Spiritual revelation.

Revelation is disruptive by definition and uncomfortable by nature. It would have been easier to move in the directions set for me since childhood by my parents—to move toward becoming the agreed-upon worldly-wise being they wanted me to be.

I see the description of the Pattern as an important learning tool for myself and my extended family, simply because it presents an integrated detail of life that is anchored in a Spiritual reality. It provides an explanation that marries science to Spiritualism. It is the evolution of faith wedded to proofs; it demands that no person or institution stands between my Core Consciousness and my human consciousness. There is no requirement for a go-between.

The Pattern is the explanation of the Word as the creator of man, of myself. As the Spiritual Word, the Pattern represents the ultimate harmony. As an expression of energy, it is the woven, complete symphony of sound whose parts make up the final integrity of a masterpiece. The Pattern is the harmonic framework upon which life on all levels expresses itself. It is the path of the Word through our reality.

The Pattern is a newer description of an older phenomena of integrated systems. These systems work in common purpose to lift us from self-denial and untruth into the realm of self-realization and truth.

The descriptions, once characterized as personal redemption and salvation, are seen, through a new view of our world system, as an aspect of the Pattern, or the Word as Spirit, the expected outcome of man's individual pursuit in search of unity.

I see the Pattern not as a function of belief, but as a reflection of personal experience interpreted in the context of a directed, multifaceted Spiritual intelligence that is active in the affairs of man.

## LIFE WITHOUT A SPIRITUAL REFERENCE

In our physical maturity we have forgotten the Spiritual resources we once knew naturally and intimately as children. We are lost to the living experience of our Spiritual nature through the barriers of life. The barriers are not insurmountable; many experience a transcendent moment in their lives when all the pieces of personal reality fit exactly into the Pattern of the eternal now. Some experience a moment when they know, without explanation or proof, the eternal being of love; the moment when the boundary between Spirit and mind becomes blurred, when we bask in the radiant glow of our greater Self.

The experience of being is not reserved or limited to a few. It is a gift of Spirit that comes unannounced, often by surprise, to all. We prepare our Self for the moment of reunion, never knowing when we will achieve it, or if we ever will.

We are reflections of Spirit's conception of the ideal of man. This ideal is the original conception of the Core Consciousness, how its thoughts are made into Spirit—pure, simple, radiant in being. Without the deflections of life to obstruct our view of Self, each of us reflects the ideal of man, incorporating it through our Self, mind, and body. There are limits to the self-experience of Spirit for this simple reason: *we are not trained to be self-realized.* Our world is forever engaged in self-survival.

As the materialization of the Spiritual idea of man, we are collectively incomplete in final form, each seeking our own completion of an Ideal. We begin the journey to realization of Spirit through the crucible of material existence, without our pre-material access to the experience of Spirit as an endlessly revitalizing force.

We do benefit from its action within our bio-system, though evoking the union of Spirit to conscious being by demand is a fruitless effort in the beginning stages. We are not prepared to receive the experience of Spirit in a meaningful way by demanding it. The forced experience is often a shattering one. Preparation and discipline, connected with the purity of intent and the grace of karma, are the puzzle that we must complete before reunion with the Creator.

As beginners we lack the language and focus needed to coordinate our consciousness with the Spiritual realm. So, we rely on symbols to unite ourselves with the intent to gain Spiritual consciousness. Our systems are based on material reality. We are governed by the laws of material reality until we collect enough force and energy to move our consciousness out into the realms of supra-consciousness. We are all beginners, entertaining the possibilities of Spirit through myth and symbols.

As a society we are unprepared for the reality of the Pattern. It is unlikely we will ever really be prepared. The direct inflow of Spirit into consciousness is greeted with the full force of personality. The inflow can be healing or damaging. St. Paul found this to be true, as he was greeted by Spirit at the gates of Damascus. He saw a blinding light and was humbled to the core of his being. So enwrapped in personality and self-centeredness, the inflow of Spirit penetrated the casement of his anger and negativity, shattering the walls of his mind.

*Greeting Spirit can be as simple as saying "Hello" to a beloved friend that we have been waiting for. Then again, not everyone is ready to say hello.*

*Think then of humankind as it awaits the inflow of Spirit. As a collective being we are simply unprepared for the experience. When this happens, how many will be shattered? How many will be numbed and bewildered? How many will move inward with grace in the exhalation of Spiritual being.*

The requirement for the transformation of our culture, from its current political agendas to the agenda of Spirit, will be overwhelming and devastating. Spirit comes as fire and destruction for the unprepared.

In the meantime, the great triumph of Spirit over flesh will occur within the very small periphery of the individual experience, not as a whole in the being of our collective consciousness. The triumph of integration in Spirit will happen person to person, moment to moment, event to event.

Our religious systems, as presented and maintained in the early years of our great religions, were born of the experience of Spirit in the moments of daily living. Belief became transformed into awareness. These systems were once able to accommodate our need for Spiritual realization. Today they are not.

The monolith of religion has drifted from the personal experience of salvation and grace to the maintenance of ideology. Systems prevail where once faith was exalted.

We now stand alone, as much as those times before the sons of The Creator walked the earth and shared the joy of Spirit. We are alone.

We have forgotten the basic lessons of Spirit. Spirit enlivens our being, regenerating and revitalizing our life forces. Those whose intent is to experience Spirit again, whose eyes and hearts are focused within our Core Consciousness, are given the confidence to walk through the complexities of life with heart and humor.

In our inconsolable loss of Spiritual being, we look to those people who have breached the doors to the Spirit world through meditation, visions, and near-death experiences. We see the unique, living example of Core Consciousness's grace in their ethereal faces and calm reflections. Those of living grace are not beyond reality. Rather, they are blessed to experience symbols of our greater ideals, living pathways to our own self-realization.

The indwelling Spirit, which is activated by desire and faith, and realized by prayer, is structured by meditation and contemplation. It shines through the eyes, pouring through skin and breath, telegraphing the subtle signals of well-being and connectedness. We find to our awe that the eyes of the spiritually attuned are unglazed by comic-book realities: their attention is simply focused on Spirit as an integral part of their lives. They seem to pass beyond the aggravations, fears, and concerns that anchor us to our densest physical awareness. They step through each moment in full awareness, seeing the subtle connecting network that binds their reality with ours, and in turn with Spirit. They make clear the absolute and enervating experience of harmony a reality. It then transcends the disruptive experience of isolation—the pain of being alone—and the effect of being cut off from all others.

With the exception of those who access the indwelling Spirit, we as a people live in personal isolation within the cavern of our mind; the dark place full of mirrors and enticing entrapments. It is here where we examine, inspect, and judge our self-image for flaws and deviations from the master template constructed from forgotten childhood experiences.

It is in our unformed, traumatized minds that we evolve our life events, unrealized dreams, wins, losses, and incompletions. It is in the mind we shape personal reality without the benefit of light or understanding. We send forth pictures of happiness and well-being that are not always healthy or achievable. The mind is always childlike in its needs and wants; an unfulfilled, insatiable machine that craves gratification.

*It is in the mind—through personality—that our true Selves are revealed. They are not revealed as evil or good, but as accommodations to the irreconcilable differences between our inner being and outer self. Our internal needs and drives are immeasurably incongruent with our external reality. It is this failure to align these two disparate poles that forces disharmony, creating discontent, inappropriate behavior, and ultimately self-destruction.*

There is no hope or relief from the demands of the mind because ethical systems and moral guidelines are unanswered in the drive for self-gratification. Without the balancing influence of Spirit, we are sophisticated killers—pure survivalists, without peer. Without a guiding context of accountability to a greater whole, a higher ideal than self-fulfillment, we stand revealed. We are vulnerable to the inner beast in all our religions; its savagery can be exposed at any given moment—the walking killer that stalks undiminished.

Social systems as a whole are not sufficient to train the beastly self. There are few restraints in behavior other than those accepted in the child mind by pain and terror. Our prisons attest to this fact. Our adult controls falter before we leave the nest and become still reminders—the nuisance of flies.

Our philosophers understand the beasts within; our behaviorists define it by pain and reward. Our moralists say that man is inherently good, offering no proof other than their fellow travelers' agreement.

Our Core Consciousness as expressed through Spirit gives man control of life, making decisions our own, without the influence of others. Until then, we reap tragedy and sorrow again and again, where unfocused emotions and attitudes become the root of interpersonal disharmonies.

We are free to choose and free to act and have done so for thousands of years. Yet, we slowly feel the subtle influences exerted by the energy network of Spirit as we express our lives. Our greater senses feel the truth. Our Spiritual sentinels teach us these truths through dreams and meditations. We are not blind to the real movement of life from birth to death, but we are mostly unconscious throughout it.

Our Higher Selves are immune to persuasion, as well as the daily persuasion of our lives through the exercise of free will— the extraordinary gift of Core Consciousness that even the angelic hosts do not boast of. The Higher Self always bows before our choices, setting our destinies free to reap the fruit of our actions and thoughts.

Spirit is ruthlessly compassionate because it is a Forever Being—indestructible in nature; an uncreated reality that supersedes the limitations of life. It persists in the face of human disaster, unflinching in its purpose to educate our Self to the realities of life. Our higher Selves, our infinite Spirits, are our teachers and guides. Their wisdom shows us the path that leads through life's indecisions and untruths to the balance of life that we seek in all actions and thoughts. It points; we choose. We are the authors of our destiny.

We may live with the Higher Self as our Spiritual reference point—a fixed star in the changing Patterns of life. Alternatively, we may disregard its constant light and choose instead to be shaped by the multi-dimensional realities afforded by the bodies we live in. We are in this sense the combined consciousness of two modes, two beings—a greater total. Like a Core Consciousness, we may return to do this again and again, until one day, we tire of the game and choose to play in bigger arenas—to dance within greater visions and possibilities—the possibilities of Spirit.

It is this process of *shaping our personal reality without the benefit of Spiritual values and insights* that produces life's evils. It is the personality's inexperience at forming a co-mingled physical and Spiritual reality that lies at the root of our problems. The exterior forces that seek to mold us through deceit and domination are not the issue—our own inability to fend those forces off are the real problem.

The blind are easily led astray. Those who live in the forces of harmony and balance gain the wisdom and the power needed to break out of the Patterns of destructive karma.

*Spirit refuses to judge us* because it understands that we ourselves are our harshest judge. Spirit seeks to heal the personality through creating alignment between internal and external realities. We are afforded opportunities to transform our point of view from the finite to the infinite. Unfortunately, we judge ourselves and others by the effectiveness of our *presentation* and thus miss the truth behind reality; we are inexperienced, unwitting voyagers who must find our direction by trial and error.

*Our images—our presentations and appearances—are of no value when measured in eternity.*

We are subject to the shifting of unknown rules, guaranteeing that today's pleasure will be tomorrow's dry void. There is no hanging on, no refusing to let go, and no moving on. Resistance to the flow and ebb of our karma only accelerates the process of collecting energy debts.

That's when resistance becomes the focal point of our lives and the living expression of our tragedies.

*It is at the point of fending off the forces of change and development that we suffer the most. Fighting the inflow of Spirit is contrary to our true natures.* Resistance is a useless effort that focuses our energy onto keeping the illusory shape of reality as we know it. Soon we are inundated with negative energy, as we ourselves become a focal point, the magnet that attracts reinforcing thoughts and desires to our very beings.

Live long enough and you will see this to be true. There is no convincing the boundless arrogance of a young mind and body that revels in strength and personal energy. Let adversity and terror ride alongside them—their perspectives will change accordingly.

The grit of life's unyielding material gradually hardens to become the blunt instrument that daily beats us with the unrelenting harshness of reality. It demands an endless supply of courage and fortitude in the face of seemingly endless provocations and disruptions. We are surrounded by those like us, people who have not mastered their internal dialogue. Instead, they act out their repressed, stifled rages, angers, and passions—the stuff they keep under the iron control of fear of reprisals and condemnation. Still, their unconscious drives are more powerful than their abilities to control them, and eventually, with age and abuse, the external constraints that have sheltered us begin to crumble.

Creation hands us the tools for personal salvation, while the world hands us a life out of control—without balance or harmonious context. We know we should not be where we are, for we feel incomplete, alone, and afraid. Yet, we live in this here and now anyhow, covered in the murk of fear, indebted by obligation and inertia, spiraling out of control with the unwillingness to alter that over which we have only the ghost of control.

We, men and women of all ages, opportunities, and cultures, often see ourselves as warriors asked to fight a battle with faulty weapons and inept resources. We view ourselves as adventurers scaling the loose rock of a tall mountain. As such we think we are the epitome—not the crude ancestor to some better model.

There is no looking ahead in our lives, only reaction to the action of other reactions. We are the end we see—not the beginning. So, is it any wonder that the best of us seek the enhancement of the skills of self-survival? What else is there but that, we ask?

We demand protection from the vagaries of life, begging that we may live safely and snugly within the walls of our society—with righteous indignation. Without some Spiritual reference point, without proof of Spirit, or a sense of eternity, we are lost individually and collectively within the limitless possibilities of reality's unending shapes and thoughts—a shifting future. No moment is more secure than the last. Maybe we think there will be an adjustment for the better—or at least for the tolerable—sometime, somewhen, somewhere.

But that's not how it works.

From the point of view of this moment's reality, we don't

understand or see that we are involved in a process of learning and growth that will take thousands of years to complete, as well as rivers of tears. How can we find stability and certainty in our lives when we do not even plan beyond next week or even tomorrow?

Instead, in anguish and frustration, we resort to addictions to dull or enliven our overwhelmed senses, creating momentary euphoric highs that wash clean our fears and create islands of personal satisfaction. But even those respites are soon blown away by the crisp winds of life's changing Patterns.

These addictions—large and small—rule our lives with iron hands, proving too pervasive and insinuating for the strongest. They dedicate us to an unplanned fight, bending our best intentions to personal gratification, moments of enforced solitude and quiet, however brief.

We don't know that we are powerless in the face of an uninformed reality that is without recognition of its source. No mind or back can effectively withstand the pressures brought to bear on us by the unceasing beat and rhythm of life. There's no Total Self hidden or living that rushes forth to salvage our mangled realities. There is only you and me seeking accommodations and compromises in the greater game of Spirit.

We have forgotten, forever, that we set these rules in cooperation with Spirit. In Spirit we acknowledge the game that promptly programmed our consciousness to forget its creator. We desired to move on from the eternal bliss of Spirit and so took the material world to heart as our teacher and mentor. We forgot the basic agreements and forgot our incorruptible relationship with our Maker.

We forget all of this and wonder in turn what the reason for this madness is. Why? As pure Spirit we tread the eternal steps of sameness. We viewed from afar the struggles of our fellows and were pulled by the love that binds our Selves to the agonies and terrors experienced by other Selves. From a distance, wrapped in the womb of heaven, our fears seemed without foundation—the perfect view to life was as a game of being. The sweet call of material reality, the promise of pleasure and the gift of life beckoned us forward.

We became our own creator in this perfect vision of Spirit, and soon firmly planted our feet in the dense muck of life. Viewed from the mud, love and perfection severed us from Spirit. And there we stood, lost within the Creator, without a way to journey back.

# Chapter 6: Search for Spirit, New Consciousness

*The Pattern seeks balance at every moment, moving and rippling with changes created by decisions and actions that our species demands of us.*

### THE VISION

When we look for the precedents and evidence of who we really are, we find hints of these buried in legend and religious myth. Shift your attention from these proofs to the open discourse in the nature and place of Spirit in our lives. Look for the awakenings of Spirit in your heart and mind. Look beyond proofs and into your heart and there you will see yourself, limitless, dynamic and ever present in Self's connection to Spirit. It's all there inside of us, stuffed into a little water-filled container we call our body. Look within for what you need, trust your Higher Self to lead you to self-realization.

The mind and heart, the energetic immortal being that we are, will outlast our physical bodies. Unquestioned beliefs are as dry as old age, bitter as the taste of spoiled fruit. As we live this life we cherish the simple loving memories of our beloved. The rewards of achievement pass as the night, and we are no more, though we are all.

The human, natural-mind construct isn't one of self-management or a capacity for tolerance and balance. Rapacious in nature, driven by self-interest and survival, there is no mistaking our motivations or signals when acting outside of expanded consciousness. Impulses become dangerous and lethal as we unconsciously act out these moments of stress and fear.

The memory of who we are in Spirit shifts from an open, all-knowing vast consciousness that on birth encloses us, to an amnesiac life that seeks forgotten memories; blind men grasping the coats of blind leaders in absolute faith and trust in hope of the ephemeral wisps of good fortune we seek.

Our Higher Self Essence looks on in compassion at the play of our life, as we are created afresh from the collective substance of Self, balanced by our personal ledger sheet in the Book of Life. Again and again, Self whispers, "Try again and step this time from the illusion of material reality into the clear, healing, enervating light of Spirit." It wishes us the best in our ascent into higher consciousness.

Through the music of the spheres—in the wind, in the sound of new life, in the quiet of meditation and prayer—we hear our guides. Guardians, and voices of the long past people within these moments of simplicity, disaster and pain, joy and love. Always available, seldom heard, they speak to us every moment of our lives.

In the death of hope, the whispered beckoning sounds of Spirit's love call us forth into self-realization. We hear so faintly the healing sound of Spirit's encouragement, assuring us that for these efforts to grow, to become more than our fate has asked of us, is the real key to unlocking the closed gates of heaven

Listen then to the poetry of man's personal, unattended, masterful, and exalted struggle to know Self, and you will see that personal redemption has already been won in the timeless void of uncreated Spirit.

## LIFE WITHOUT A SPIRITUAL REFERENCE

Love is the foundation of the Pattern of life, needed to build our courage for another day of struggle.

We live without reference to Spiritual values without being grounded in the surety and guarantee of a Spiritual reference point (a place of beginning and ending and the place we may return home to). There is no up or down. Nor is there a beginning or end. Without a sure, clear reference point, our lives evaporate into meaningless symbols. There is little comfort or value if we face life's humiliating experiences unaided by faith and the living experience of Spirit.

As Spirit works out its unique destiny in the material world, death takes us into its heart—not as an enemy, but as an ending to a song that has sung its course.

Arriving in our new body—fresh in Spirit and pure in intent—we begin again. Born anew in shapeless personality, we twist and mold reality to achieve the lofty ambitions of our dreams. Each life begins our life again, and again.

Our supposition is that we are dropped whole from heaven into humanity. A selected righteous few are allowed to pass the heavenly inquisitors and proceed through heaven's gate.

In the evolution of consciousness, unintegrated components of Self are drawn from the vast creative motif of the Pattern. We hear our Creator in moments of simplicity and love, in disaster and pain.

*We live not knowing the reasons for our birth, life, and death until we have transitioned into Spirit.*

## FINDING REALITY IN SPIRIT

Unsure how to place the validity of our experience in the day-to-day reality of our own life without a tangible spiritual Essence—we live a life without a Spiritual reference point. If we don't believe in our own experience, why should anyone else? Man seeks Self in his own way and is ready and available to believe and experience the touch of heaven's wind.

Reality is found in Spirit as we question the beliefs that are the glue to our reality. Questioning is the fire that brings the pot to boil, that sparks inquisition and encourages political murder.

Spirit visits the mind open to possibilities and potential. Spirit is open to the mind that turns inward to perceive the logic of man as forced, confined by the constraints of the five senses.

Higher Self operates in inexplicable ways unfathomable to most people. We say and ask for the directions to heaven, thinking it is reachable in the directions given to us by human lips. Failing this test, we quit—discouraged. We fail to remember that each of us is invited to seek the love of Spirit and its power to function fully in our lives—to be transformed into a Spiritual prototype. The Pattern of Spiritual consciousness intervenes in each life. There is no provable doorway, path, or step that will infallibly take us to Core Essence's realm, we seek our own destiny.

Beliefs are the physical manifestations of the basic principles available to us through prayer and intuition. As individuals, we create the pathway to Higher Self. At that moment of truth, when knowing we have failed in the final chapter of each life, we judge ourselves and find, in higher consciousness, that Spirit listens in perfect understanding. Failure is life guiding us to a fuller participation in life.

Returning from intensely personal visions of Spiritual realities, mystics, saints, gurus all have explained our Higher Self as an all-encompassing force manifested as light and sound in an integrated harmony of Being, part of a Pattern of super reality underling all consciousness.

## LIFE WITHOUT SPIRIT

Our lives pass in a brief span of time. Our helplessness in the face of personal tragedy and misfortune is real. Our sense of being without guidance is real, yet living in denial of Spirit buries our experience, leaving us at the gate of our hearts. Without a Spiritual reference, the interior structures we build are as those built on sand.

## DECEMBER 3–4, 2021: A HEALING WITH REMOVAL OF AN ENERGY ATTACHMENT AND A FOLLOW-UP VISIT

John, a friend, sent me a text saying he wanted to remove his attachment he had named "Ray." This is the first time, after a year of discussion, I'd heard him name his parasitic attachment. This was not good. How can you willingly remove a close, intimate friend? Or advisor? A source of the emotional juice in your life?

I became very alarmed with his personal battle and my assumptions that cherishing the presence of "Ray," an accelerating process of dealing with depression and anxiety, produced bursts of anger, and would accelerate the energetic parasite's presence. I had spent time reviewing what I knew and saw about John's energetic attachment.

It was very different than others that I'd removed. I decided it was a hereditary attachment, which is an attachment that had resided in the host and the host's family for hundreds of years. These long-term familial attachments are passed from the Mother to the child. Usually, the recipient is noticed to have mood swings, constant depression, or an inclination to addiction.

I talked about the removal process and was advised to proceed without John's cooperation. I did not want to heal while the Host and the attachment joined in a struggle to stay intact. I said to John there was no need to get me involved in a healing until he was ready to cooperate in the removal process, whether conscious or unconscious. It did not matter.

With his text message asking for removal, I suspected John had had enough and was ready to have the energy parasite removed. I chose this time period to proceed, assuming the Host was either asleep or fatigued, a healing version of anesthesia.

I found embedded in John's body a visible presence, an energetic gray thick-skinned body whose liquid sack floated above his right shoulder and then moved with a slow-motion roll of fat layers whose lower half fully penetrated John's body.

The attachment was a thick cord or tendrils that penetrated the nervous system's complex wiring. This one had had a long time to grow and embed itself. The tendrils were affecting emotions, thoughts, producing depression and rages, amplifying drinking and sexual desires.

These attachments matched John's energetic body to easily feed on his body's life system and etheric body's structure. Without compatibility, the reception of the attachment/parasite will be problematic. Viable hosts are sought life after life in a multitude of potential hosts. It seems that the match is made secure by the genetic structure of the Host's DNA.

The attaching energy parasite is a very sophisticated primal attachment. These energetic attachments have been feeding off humans from the beginning of known time. There have been five successive developments of animal consciousness to the perfected higher consciousnesses of the dominant species.

The healing started with accepted body signals. The energy I was channeling created a clear signal to begin. With my energetic directions to Spirit, the attachment was flooded with light, a white light with a yellowish tinting and some purple and blue streams into the nervous system of the Host, the light energy rocking the parasite from is attachment to the nerve sheathing.

As the energy connected and held the nerves, they were gently, but implacably, pulling the exposed sack slowly outwards, and continued to rock the connected tendrils and pull these out slowly. I had a great concern about how the attachment was embedded. Tearing "Ray" was out of the question. Disintegrating the energy through energy blasts could damage the integrity of John's energy and nerve system.

I called out to my guardian angel, Priscus, who showed up and stood by me. Though his light emanations charged the body of the Host, and he held the sack, he would do no more. He is very prickly about intervening or helping in my healing work. If I can do the work, he won't get involved, and to date I have finished what was needed.

This healing was very complicated, so many moving parts, so I sent the Tre' Cha' sphere into the body and it began snipping the connectors of the attachment's tendrils from the nervous system. This was a very delicate and complicated network; these tendrils had been established for more than 60 years. Real damage to the nerves, from the etheric body linked to the physical body, could have been permanently damaging to the Host's body.

As the attachment was removed it sought out my energy body to re-attach itself. My defensive system reacted, as the gift ring of the Master and my House brightened, and repulsed the attempt. I could see the identity of the attachment as a symbol of being. This was surprising. The attachment was a conscious entity, not the mindless parasite I had imagined.

It was now fighting for dominance against the flow of energy. I finally pulled off the entity attachment (it was a life-form I had not seen before, self-aware and feeding on one body after another from the inception of life). I pushed it out and away from its host, then went back in to clean up its remnants and close its entry point. The Host would be disoriented for a few days and emotionally reactive.

I withdrew. This work was done. The Host would need to be protective against a new attachment. Removal of the energy attachment would be like losing a body part. Usually, the loss is deeply felt in a long-term sense as sadness and emptiness for one like this. The need to shield energetically the Host from the attachments is critical to avoid new attachments. The energetic body until healed will be a target for other like-minded energetic parasites.

I shifted back to home base which was fast and did not require much deceleration of the energetic (astral) body. Coming back was a vibrational jolt from high speed to the slower moving physical body. Tired but satisfied I went back to sleep.

## DECEMBER 6, 2021: FOLLOW-UP

I woke from sleep this morning with an impulse to check on the condition of the person who I had completed a removal process on 12-3-21. The pull was something not to be put off. I shifted there using my entire energetic body. Healing using solely consciousness is not as effective.

My arrival (instantaneous as it was) brought me to the body for a closer look. I went down into the location of the attachment, noticed the scarring in the etheric body, and sought any presence of the attachment the person identified as "Ray." People who have long-term infestations tend to personalize and build a working relationship with the attachment. The attachment pulls emotional energy while presenting a "helpful" energy in return. This can go on throughout the person's life. In this situation the attachment was what I call a hereditary entity that had moved through generations of the family.

More likely the person has a DNA structure that appeals to

and fits the needs/wants of the attachment. The person who is quietly suffering from this kind of attachment fully believes there is a beneficial and reciprocal relationship between the two. It also means the attachment has had a lifetime to burrow into the nervous system of the victim.

There is no beneficial relationship. There is feeding on a host with the feeding entity soothing (temporarily) their host. Many hosts are prone to addictions such as to physical and sexual energy. Often the host has an addictive tendency that leads to alcoholism.

I scanned the body and saw that there were traces of the attachment's tentacles. Unlike what I have seen before, the tentacles had a fibrous appearance. The fibers were in a growth mode. Self-replicating the embedded entity, these would regrow themselves over the remaining years of the host's life. Not good.

Due to my lack of experience in traversing the layout of the nervous system, I called out to my guide Tre' Cha', an old and potent energy sphere, for help. Tre' Cha' knew how to move into the nerves and remove the fibers. It also allowed me to see its work, and what I say were strings of fibrous tendrils that were moving and pushing themselves to rejoin into a new entity. Stunning visuals.

The Tre' Cha' went to work, isolating the growth carefully to not damage the host in the retrieval process. I watched enraptured if not enthralled by the process that eventually resulted in the embedded tendrils removal. The body was scanned again, and nothing remained. The host would be susceptible to later attachments if a vigil was not taken to protect him. Or he would continue to energetically shield himself. Habits and accommodations experienced in a lifetime need a diligent care to prevent the attachments or others of its kind from returning. I returned to home base and thought out the experience. The attachment had shown up in my personal space and tried to attach to my energy field. Good luck with that. As a precaution, I went to the location on the 36$^{th}$ ring where the majority of my total Self resided and experienced a thorough healing.

The healing device looks like a white Christmas wreath with Italian lights of many colors, flashing and glowing within its wreath. I was highly amused but settled down as I experienced a deeper healing than ever before. What works, works! On waking I felt refreshed and attachment clean. (If there had even been a successful implant).

This attachment had run through hundreds of years in this family. It was strong, extremely intuitive, and pissed off at me. And its Host. This had to be taken seriously. Again, I sent it into the Light, but not surprisingly it disappeared, probably to create mischief in another Host.

Our personal awareness expands and flowers if we remain open to the creative flow of Spirit. Sometimes we see the true intent of Spirit as it moves through and in us.

Spirit is enriching our energetic body, adding a cohesiveness to life that no other force or energy can replace or substitute. It is often said that money and power cannot buy happiness. It's more than this: only Spirit can rejuvenate a broken heart, give courage to a faltering Spirit, or let you enjoy the satisfaction of spending the money you have.

The Creative Forces of Spirit are unconcerned that we may disrupt their flow or work. They are impervious to our demands for attention and cannot be bought with prayer. They are simply tools used to open the gateway of our awareness. There is a Pattern, a plan and a strategy that will enfold man into the reality of Spirit. These things become clearer and more evident as we reach for greater consciousness, striving to press our understanding beyond that of the senses.

As a part of a greater communal entity, we discuss ideas and co-create on a Spiritual level. We do not stand alone; our Spirits converse with others even as our minds are closed to the glory of this exchange. Through the manifestation of grace, Spirit slowly drags us kicking and screaming into the greater reality of Core Essence.

We live within a vast network of Spiritual forces that thrive in a Pattern of Spiritual evolution of consciousness. They take no heed of our denials or misery, continuing to nourish us in peace or adversity.

The Pattern is the movement, strategy, and goals of the creative force of Spirit as it works to move man forward to his natural position in the Spiritual hierarchy. It is the framework of man's Spiritual growth: a practical guide of how-to in the working relationship between man and Spirit. It is called the Pattern here because a Pattern is the guide, a template for all forms of consciousness and the outline of where and how we also may create.

The working of the Pattern is called Patterning, which is the actual direction and cooperation between the creative forces and each of us, both individually and as a whole. When we accept Patterning as a way of viewing reality, we perceive the fundamental abstraction we call life. The driving forces shape our reality.

As in any creative effort, the Pattern is neither a rule nor a command. It is, a shifting arrangement of life's energies as they seek to conform to the direction of the creative forces. The Pattern directs, suggests, and pushes these creative forces into precise formations of energy, into a shifting energy relationship that is designed to nourish the growth of the earth and its inhabitants. All forms of consciousness use the force and direction of the Pattern to reinforce and support their efforts to join with Spirit. Unfettered from the debilitating effect of fear, we become joyous co-creators in the unfolding of life.

Reality it is a shifting Pattern of variety and depth. This Pattern can is used to work in harmony with Spirit's creative priorities in the evolution of life on this planet. By accepting the Pattern's essence, we gain Spiritual freedom.

Man stands on the brink of the New Age as a partner in creation; there is much work to be done. Listen carefully to the small, still voice within. In time, the unfolding of the design of the Pattern will transcend belief and move into your reality as a direct Spiritual experience. In truth, we stand forever in hand with our creator.

# Chapter 7: Inherent Resources

*The triumph of our integration in Spirit happens person to person, moment to moment, event to event.*

### CYCLES OF LIFE, DEATH AND LIFE

We die in flesh to move onto Spirit. We die in Spirit to move into flesh. It is like visiting a friend for a lengthy vacation, then returning home, glad to be in a familiar nurturing place we are comfortable with.

Death is a gift of the body to our Selves, as we pass from here to there. The departure is filled with regret and sadness. An unknown longing pulls us forward into the light and bathes us again in its rejuvenating stream of pure energy, purified as the dense cloak of the physical world burns away. The memories holding us back from the light are released. The burning emotions that twist our minds from life dissolve as energy dissipates from us—as life does from flesh.

Death is an enervating freedom which is not experienced in its blinding radiance in this life; it is life experienced as a new reality. Without Spirit, we are stone. As we weep the tears of death in life, we lose life and its fitful release through death.

Born again in a shapeless future—and placed here with the

accumulation of thoughts, emotions, gifts, and talents—our fractured Spirits are covered over in fresh paint. We wait for the triggers of karma that soon come our way.

We cannot partake in the mystery of Self that shows us as a location of being, a place where Spirit intertwines with flesh forming a unique, vibrant, dynamic being. We are unexposed to the concept of man as a member of an evolving species which is nearing a transition point from the material to the Spiritual. We fear to see ourselves as bridges of light; conduits of Spirit from source to being.

Our supposition is that we are dropped whole from heaven into humanity. This limited, stunted image of Self quiets all active perceptions of reality.

### JANUARY 14, 2021, 5:00 A.M.: MEDITATION ON SOURCE

This morning I took a rather long trip to the source of life through a meditative process.

Relaxing, speeding up the frequency of my energetic body, affirming my intent to go forward with purpose, I sat back and waited to begin.

I moved my consciousness from here to there, a location of no time, no past or future, no ego. Timeless. It is a location of shimmering, black, unmanifested creative potential. I expanded my energy to the edges of the galaxy, including all things and nothing. As I expanded, the black light embraced me. I could create here or do nothing. This space had no agenda, strategy, achievement. No program to follow. Again, timeless.

I spent a little time there, reviewing what I could create, and saw within my energy field all of the unmanifested thought forms and created energy I had stored up since my beginning. None were actualized. They were there waiting for my intention to manifest them. It was like looking at a junkyard of lost dreams, unrealized ambitions, failures in coherent thought... a record of the wasted energy I had spun off from myself.

I resolved to return with a sweeper and pan and clean up the mess. For source to manifest, there needed to be space and order.

Then I stepped through to pure source, a palpable weight of unfocused, unformed energy. I thought of the one place in my experience that held a beauty and timelessness I had never met before. It was a small glade near the Park in the City of Lights. Rich green grass, ringed by oak trees. Ah hah, the druids peek out from the perfectly dense growth. I found a stone bench and sat, meditating the beginning of who I was, a high priest in Atlantis, a keeper of the earth's core energy, the energy that powered cities and life. A Buddhist monk studying and teaching scripture in China, then a monk in solitary seclusion in a cave high in the mountain ranges of Tibet. Yes, this past life was the key to my current manifestation in time. He saw forwards and backwards, and saw, in all of the riches of learning, knowledge, mastery of physical forces, that I was missing one key experience. Emotion. All my lives before that monk were intellectual. There was little emotion. Every life touched on or was lived in a religious environment.

He decided to redirect my/his soul to embrace emotion and learn its manifestation in the uncounted times to come. I/Monk passed into the new life and there he engineered my energy body to experience emotion in its full blossom. As a result, in my next series of lives, I was a bit slow-witted, very emotional, and prone to bouts of aggression. Viking, soldier on a shield wall, marauder, killer, seeker of gold. This lasted for more than a thousand years as I began slowly to control the emotions through learning and creative arts. Discipline and focus using emotion drove me forward.

I ended up in Rome, a soldier, and a convert to the new Christian religion. I died in the Rome amphitheater bearing witness to Christ. My life from then to today has been a progression of experiences in Self-awareness that continues to give witness, unknown to me, to the driving forces that compelled me forward. I regained lost experience, a wealth of education, my physical and mental discipline as a royal assassin (killer on behalf of a King, I rediscovered talents for far-seeing, energetic healing, and gained many spiritual allies).

I saw my beginning and my finish on earth. Forwards and backwards. Every detail. And now was accepted back into Spirit through these experiences.

Then I moved forward to the Gathering, as different forms of consciousness, to watch the birth of a new soul-consciousness on earth. I saw the ending of Atlantis, the rebuilding of the planet, the introduction of man's prototype. This moved forward to now. The tensions induced by the pressure of the birth of a new state of being threw societies into war, turmoil, until a massive nuclear war again killed most of humanity. I saw the earth was cleansing itself of the pestilence of man and reshaping herself for the new consciousness.

I saw that, going forward, more and more children will come into life without the cloaking of past lives. With wisdom and knowledge. They will be seeds of the new generations that will lead man out of the constant recycling of lives into cooperative stewardship.

I saw that for the remainder of my time here I would continue to learn about and manifest source. My other work was to learn about the creative source of the clear light of love. Each had its powerful contribution to life, and each was available for me to know and shape for myself. This is a personal mission/goal: to honor both black source energy and the pure colorless light of creativity and love.

I returned to the City of Lights and stood looking out into the beauty of the park with new eyes. When I turned 31, my guide and Helper since my first experience in consciousness travel was there. This time she was out of the guide uniform and cloaked in a flowing, white light. I was surprised but with her it is better to stay silent. I looked closely and remembered her face from many encounters in the Spiritual realm. I got it. She beamed before I spoke. "No. 1, you are my Guardian Angel!" She nodded and smiled. I felt emotion at this and wanted to hug her. She did not allow that to happen! Then another connection was made. I said, "You are my future Self! You are here to protect me and eventually bring me home." She smiled again and winked out.

*It occurs to me that any energy shielding/cloaking that manifests in the physical/flesh-bound layer of reality is dependent upon and subject to the dominant will in the immediate physical area. Will is that which calls forth and manifests creative or destructive intent in the physical realm.*

*Regarding large area coverage, I see that there are very few flesh-bound sentients, if any right now, that can individually master the energy and will to deploy and maintain such an energy structure. That this might require the will of a concerted group effort is, in my estimation, dead on. I believe it is something that humans used to do within their small band-sized communities, almost instinctively, and that it has also been ritualized to some effect.*

*So, if one were to capture and manipulate (don't take that negatively) the will of a large group of people over a broad physical area, anchored individually across the space, a very effective energetic shield with physical level effects could be created and maintained. In fact, just about anything is possible when the wills of many individuals blend with unified intent. It's kind of the point of all Creation.*

## SEARCHING FOR SPIRIT

Our culture vigorously pursues technology as the remedy for the unexplained, the uncontrollable. It places its mechanistic, unresponsive values as the underpinning structure to the formative concepts of our religious and aesthetic models. In the process of underrating and diminishing the unbridled creativity of the human Spirit, we drive ourselves further from the attainment of super reality into the confined spaces of shackled minds.

Love acts as the foundation to build the courage needed for one more day of effort and struggle. Where does love come from other than us, or from the other side of the human experience—the Spiritual side? The biological side is motivated only by the forces of survival. Yet, it is managed ultimately by the apparent intangible of emotion as expressed by the human Spirit.

## INTERFACE BETWEEN SPIRIT AND MAN

*Our Higher Self is sensed and felt as though
it were of the earth, not some Spiritual realm.*

## THE PATTERN'S COMPOSITION

The Pattern is composed of varying degrees of energy frequencies of consciousness that exist in different dimensions; some beyond the four dimensions attributed to man, including sight, smell, sound, and time. It is like looking at a multi-dimensional chess game placed on clear plastic sheets.

The active aspects of the Pattern are the energy frequencies represented in different individual and group energies of sentient species. Sentient is defined here as a conscious self-aware species. Because of the active nature of their consciousness, self-aware species are able to interact with Spirit as well directly. This

## Chapter 7: Inherent Resources

corresponds to their personal and group needs—the energies required to assure the upliftment of their species.

Natural Patterns and urges are a demonstration of the wiring of this species that assures perpetuation along inherent pathways. You and the fellows in your group will probably act in the same manner given a fixed set of stimuli. This coding is a natural and important security system that we cannot short-circuit, and can only overcome in unique cases. The wiring inherent in man's progression to full self-awareness insists that he pay more attention to bodily survival—sleeping, eating, and procreating.

These tendencies and inclinations are factors accounted for in the evolution of our participation in the Pattern. Our built-in tendencies as a species in relationship to particular types of stimuli are programmed into the Pattern for the protection of our species. There is very little concern for us as individuals. If we are indestructible, cannot die a permanent death, and are inheritors of Core Essence's creations, where is the concern? From Spirit's point of view in examining the trends within the Pattern, it is not surprising to see that man is wholly predictable. There are very few surprises, and the course of our destiny can be laid out fairly accurately.

As the Pattern seeks balance, this results in a fundamental change to the working of the Pattern in all aspects of our lives. This change isn't just about a way of life or means of earning money for food and shelter. It is a change of energy frequency.

Our bodies and perception of reality shift from physical-based to Spiritual-based. It will happen quickly, and in a sense, violently. The world around you won't be the same anymore. Will we want it differently once the transition or next step in upliftment has occurred? Life will go on, but it will be much different. Our reference points will be changed, and we will walk a new global reality.

Our lives—its content, the quality of our relationships, the circumstances of our existence—are all symbolic representations of our activity within the Pattern. Much as we would like to think that our achievements in life or Spiritual attainments are reflected in the Pattern, the fact is our physical reality is the net result of our activities within the Pattern. The Creative Intelligence does not view us as John or Jane Smith, doctor, lawyer, president, or whatever; it sees us as representations of energy potential.

The distance between us and our Higher Selves is our frequency and dimension within the Pattern. We are active on multiple levels because our egos are parts of our total Self, or Core Essence, which resides in unfettered Spirit within the Pattern. The Self, or ego we know and have come to learn about, that expresses needs and desires in its physical residence—our bodies—is an aspect of our total Selves. It is much like a hologram that has been shattered into pieces yet retains a total picture in each piece.

It is unrealistic to expect the unfettered potential of our Core Essence to be crammed into the limited potential of the current human version of our reality. As time passes and we move closer to the Higher Self ideal of expressing Spirit, more and more of our potential will be utilized.

## CORE ESSENCE

The Core Essence, or aspect of our Selves that resides in total freedom within the Pattern, manages and pushes all of the other aspects of ourselves towards unification. Remember that in the context of Spirit there is no time—beginning or end—just an endless now. Our Core Essence resides in that environment of endless now and has access to the energy of creation.

We each have a power potential that is immeasurable. Core Essence manipulates and nurtures all of our evolving Selves simultaneously, direct us to the ultimate goal of unification with Spirit. One day we will return to the Spirit to remain forever in its dynamic creative state. In the meantime, our Core Essence sends us forth into creation to experience and learn all of the aspects of the physical world.

As we near completion, we are bonded to the myriad personalities that have lived before us, but that occur in the Spirit's mind simultaneously. Imagine it this way: after years of struggle, joy, and Spiritual upliftment, at some point you will very naturally begin to remember all of the lives that you lived here on earth. The remembering will occur quickly, or slowly.

There is profound rejoicing when one of us makes the transition from four-dimensional beings (sight, sound, smell, time) to multi-dimensional personalities working for the growth of man as a species—not just the forwarding of our own interests and concerns.

Remembering is a key step in participation within the Pattern since the process brings us closer to unification with our Higher Selves, or that which we perceive as Higher Self, or the Higher Self within. The process takes lifetimes of diligent work and can begin or finish at any time in our lives.

Cosmic consciousness, which is like placing our awareness in hyperspace for a short period, is the final crowning of a series of events in expanded consciousness. As a crowning human event, it presages unification with the Core Essence at all levels of the Pattern. It is, in effect, the beginning of the end of our stay in the physical world, the heralding of a final transition from the physical to the Spiritual.

# CHAPTER 8:
# CORE ESSENCE, NEURAL NETWORK OF CONSCIOUSNESS

*The Pattern is impregnated with the spark of creation,*
*that essential energy that begins life and ends it.*

### PLACEMENT OF A SOUL WITHIN THE PATTERN

The Pattern is the neural network of the Creative Intelligence. Essence, our Spirit, uses the creative aspect of framing and linkage to direct and manage the flow-through of its intent into materialization.

The notion of the manifestation of man, or the events of man through his material and super-conscious reality, as an unexplained occurrence diminishes the dynamic structure of reality. It places the event of our being in the place of myth and fairy tale. The Spiritual events of man in both personal and cultural contexts are not happenstance; they are the planned expression of Spirit.

The Pattern is outside of time or space. It does not need verification or belief. It is the underlying structure of all reality. Its localized expression is set-up to assist man in the process of evolving from a material being into a Spiritual being. The myriad expressions of reality are reflections of Spirit's intent to push man through the barriers of dimensional consciousness into the ever-expanding levels of open consciousness.

As we progress through the aspects of consciousness—from the most fundamental, natural being in the world of primitive reality to the ongoing expressions of higher consciousness—we move closer to an awareness of the Pattern as the driving reality of all expressions of life.

We become co-creators in our personal expression of the unfolding of our consciousness the closer we move in awareness to the Pattern. It is the nature of being to expand into the inclusion of life as a part of our personal reality. So, we gain awareness of the Pattern and its relationship to our being as we include more and more of the infinite expressions of reality.

It is easier to liken the Pattern to the Creator's neural network of Core Essence's Being. Each life is a spark of energy residing in the body of Core Essence. We are conscious beings connected by lines of energy and responsive to the thought of our source, aware of our individual reality, yet never knowing the scope of our individual mission because we fear to venture beyond our contained, defined realities.

Earth itself is only a single-layered reality out of many. Life as we know it exists within one of seven distinct layers of reality. The life within each layer corresponds to a specific rate of vibration of energy. Some forms of life are slower than ours, so we see and feel them as dense materials. Others are faster, so we catch only glimpses of them as light and shadow. Some we can only see as fleeting movements of individual consciousness.

The Pattern contains the interface from the ethereal to the physical, as it slows down its rate of vibration or frequency to a pitch that is conducive to healthy life.

The perception of the Pattern works in the same manner. Through prayer and meditation, we seek to establish a channel of understanding with the Spirit. We are either accepted conditionally or in whole or are rejected. Why? Spirit only manifests in a vehicle of the corresponding energy rate; a vehicle that is willing and capable to bear the shift in frequency.

In reuniting with the intent of the Pattern, we find fulfillment, a harmony and blending of energy found in following the natural course of life as it takes us effortlessly to our destination—our destiny—as we know it in our current form. We mesh with the active intent of the Creative urge. We understand, possibly for the first time since treading the path of creation, the absolute sense of fulfillment in doing that thing which we find most right in our heart.

## THE PATTERN'S COMPOSITION

Our Soul is bound into place within the Pattern. We move on and within lines of creative energy much like luminous strings, a curvilinear grid of overlaying creative energy. The pieces of who we are move and interact along these lines of force, this force being, by its own inherent nature, the energy configurations of who we are, locked within the frequency at which they vibrate. There are large and small varying degrees of sentience and intelligence. Some are more flexible and some move faster within the Pattern than others.

There is no barrier or limitation of those representative energies that operate in Spirit, or free-formed energy configurations. Non-embodied human Spirits—those people who are not in the physical—are the interface between the Creative Intelligence that guides the movements of energies throughout the Pattern. The relationships of these multi-dimensional energy forms are based on their location and contribution to the Pattern, according to their unique frequency and energy composition.

The driving force of the Pattern is powered by the relationship between intent, thought for us, and the component energy aspects of the co-creators in each Pattern layer. We are valued for our contribution of energy to the Pattern more than anything else. This takes away the "destiny" aspect claimed by many individuals who profess access to the human Pattern.

There is in fact no "human" Pattern. Rather, there is a layer of the Pattern that corresponds to the frequencies specific to the perceivable aspect of personal reality. Entering the Pattern is like overlooking a cloud layer composed of moving colors, representing the intricacies of the Pattern's layered energies.

We are what we radiate energetically. We radiate what we've become. It is the valuation of our energy contribution to each other that places us on the "honor roll" of the Pattern, not words or promises. When we sum up our contribution to the Pattern at the end of our lives, we see an un-scrolling of our actions, thoughts, and love—not a litany of awards and titles. In the final analysis, energy tells—nothing else.

The most intelligent and flexible co-creators within the Pattern are not human in genus, or especially representative of matter. The human domain is one of thousands of representative life-forms within the Pattern. What of aliens and angelic beings? Aliens are not "alien" to the Pattern. Rather, they are representative energy Patterns that in turn make contributions to the Pattern. Looking into the Pattern, one sees very different energy configurations. We could classify some as human. Not all.

On a higher order of self-awareness such as man, the direction is conscious and is directed towards a path of greater self-awareness. Lower order self-aware species tend to act collectively in their urge to grow and follow the basic programming that is wired into their genetic codes. This wiring includes gene traits and evolutionary trends towards self-protection first, then self-awareness. It is the accumulation of the species as they grow from a basic form to much more complex entities.

On the face of things, there appears to be a tremendous

amount of pressure on us to conform to the flow and intricacies of the Pattern. Yet, the opposite is true. The Pattern deals with dynamic changes in its flow, such as man's constant flip-flopping regarding his decisions and actions. The Pattern is adjusting to accommodate for these delays and changes in intent. It seems to all work smoothly. We all somehow seem to avoid destroying ourselves. Dictatorships do seem to eventually fail, and generally we move on in life, a little worn, seldom changed.

The Pattern adjusts to these considerations from the macro to the micro, expressing "as above, so below," saying in effect no sparrow falls from the sky without the knowledge of the Creative Intelligence. Of course, it is easy to ask, "What is the point of our lives, the tragedy and anguish, the senseless violence?"

# Chapter 9:
# Expressions of the Pattern

*The Pattern is the underpinning design of life itself.*

## ACCESSING CREATIVITY

The Pattern looks like an overlay of different colors framed by a vast grid composed of luminous, softly glowing, white lines of energy, as perceived by our extrasensory perceptions. Each color reflects the real energy output of all living beings, their thoughts, intent, emotions, and actions. More than a bioelectrical field affected by magnetic shifts and different brain and body activities, the Pattern is the underpinning of life itself. It is the materialized thought of the creative sources we access. We build our realities upon the Pattern, using it as a template for creating our realities.

The Pattern flows from the creative source as an energy wave. Slowing in speed and energy, it creates the seeds of life within its energy spectrum as it moves simultaneously from itself into itself; a paradox of something new and something finished. The Pattern as we perceive it isn't the exclusive expression of material reality. Instead, it is an endless string of realities that respond, each in turn, to the vibration of the energy wave wherever it is manifesting at that time.

Each phase of this energy wave, by its nature the first expression of creation, seeds life without bias or thought. It is the very stuff—the raw material—of creation. It is the legion of completed life-forms following the wave that brings order to the uncontrolled life that springs forth from its passage. Life as we know it is only one of the countless forms that are created from the Pattern, but our evolution isn't uncontrolled. We are the managed creations of other life-forms whose existence is suggested, and whose realities are dimly perceived. Yet, it is essential to our final move back up through the wave to our source—the source of all life.

Each intersection of this vast energy grid is a mosaic of color and light, a living flow of energies produced by the life-forms inhabiting their section of the grid. Every section of the Pattern is impregnated with the spark of life, that essential creative energy that begins life and ends it. The earth—our earth which is one of many realities bunched together—is itself an integral component of the Pattern. It is a living being reacting to the forces and thoughts imposed upon it by its inhabitants in a holistic manner.

The intersections of energy flowing, sourced from the original energy wave that created the potential of our separate realities, bind the Pattern into a cohesive whole. Each intersection is an expression of creative intent; a clear signal of how reality is structured in order to manifest itself.

### THE PATTERN'S MANAGERS

The intelligence, or mind overseeing the working and unfolding of the Pattern, is a Spiritual hierarchy that uses the flow of energies as a neural network of points that disburse energy to predetermined locations. It is much like our bodies, which when faced with the threat of infection, release white blood cells to consume or destroy the invader.

The driving force of the Pattern is the intent of the Creative Forces—their master plan. As such, it is a co-creator in the evolution of life and Spirit for the forward movement of man in the actualization of his destiny.

In the realm where Spirit moves freely, and where energy is manipulated by intent, the realm where Spirit meets flesh is where frequency thins or is dampened from one end and increased from our end. There the interaction between the Spiritual and physical worlds becomes more vigorous. It is a fact that the basic elements of our world can be manipulated and fractured by machines. The Spiritual Intelligence manipulates physical reality to its own ends in much the same way.

The only restraint in this free manipulation is the overriding dictate that Spirit must respect man's gift of free will. Just as a painter shades the nuances of our lives through art, Spirit will not actively or frivolously interfere in our judgments and actions.

**USING ENERGY AS INTENT**

In seeking to manifest itself, Spirit expresses itself as energy. Yet, this energy is neither formless nor without direction. The creative urge of the Spirit is formed and delivered by thought in its totality, then expressed through intent. Intent is the force and direction of the creative urge and is the aspect of the creative will that ultimately manifests as life. Spirit through this force of will inserts its unique imprint of Self into the Pattern, giving it a form and direction that corresponds to its own energy Pattern.

Energy at the level of creation transcends chaos. It is formed deliberately and precisely to the needs and desires of the Pattern in conformance with the direction of that which has already been set into motion. This governing impulse allows for individual adjustments to the movement and intent of the Pattern but stops any larger tampering with its design. A shift in direction requires a level of force and intent that exceeds the energy potential of the Pattern's managers. It is an action that is exclusive to the Creator.

## CORE ESSENCE

The Core Essence, or aspect of our Selves that resides in total freedom within the Pattern, manages and pushes all of the other aspects of ourselves towards unification. Remember that, in the context of Spirit, there is no time, beginning or end—just endless now. Our Core Essence resides in that environment of endless now and has access to the energy of creation. That is why we have a power potential that is unmeasurable.

The Core Essence manipulates and nurtures all our evolving Selves simultaneously, directing us towards its ultimate goal of unification with Spirit. One day we will return to the Spirit to remain forever in its dynamic creative state. In the meantime, the Core Essence, our Higher Selves, sends us forth into creation to experience and learn all of the aspects of the physical world—letting us do our thing, make mistakes, learn, grow, and mature. We do this through seemingly countless lifetimes in physical and non-physical realities.

## INFLUENCES

*The actualization of intent puts you on the*
*level of a Creator within the Pattern.*

## THE FIRST CAUSE

The Pattern is a flow of energy set into motion by the First Cause, or Core Consciousness, for purposes and reasons that are beyond anyone's ability to grasp. It is difficult to express the point of view that there is no reason, that the universe simply is.

This point of view is endorsed by agnostics to help explain the apparently senseless violence and aggressions that occur daily. Scientists who support the mechanistic approach to life use

## Chapter 9: Expressions of the Pattern 119

science's unfolding technology—such as the Big Bang Theory, the Laws of Entropy, and other scenarios—to support a universe strictly subject to natural laws.

Creation, as it sparked, developed the breeding ground for evolving sentience, and being experimental in nature, it selected life-forms of all levels of intelligence, awareness, and dimension. Life occurs as energy coalesces into unique forms. To suggest that matter as we know it—people, animals, rocks, and such—is the sole expression of the Creative Mind effectively boxes our perception of reality into a simple four-dimensional room, where nothing other than the expected occurs.

Viewing man and other sentient species as multi-dimensional beings, occurring simultaneously with other-dimensional energy occurrences, gives a richness of explanation that defies orthodoxy. The image of Core Consciousness, a kindly old white man in a flowing robe, or a demonic woman with multiple arms, gives way to an indescribable intelligence that acts on our behalf in a master plan. This master plan functions to uplift our species and others to the level of awareness of the Creative Intelligence, to become Creator-like in our manipulation of reality. Don't worry about this happening too quickly.

The Pattern is the guiding force of reality as it occurs in all its dimensions of creativity. Creation needs a great management team. Consequently, the archetypal beings we know as angels were produced. They are really the Pattern's management group, reporting directly to the Creator for direction. Angels, in effect, live permanently in Spirit. They have no need to take the form of lower frequency beings, though they do for special occasions or if an on-the-spot fix is required. As embodiments of the Creative Mind, angels exist as pure, unadulterated energy. This is as it should be, for managing the Pattern isn't easy. The sentient species and the earth alone require seven full-time archangels, whose limitless access to energy keeps our reality, time and space in order.

## CREATING ENERGY DEBTS

Karma is a popularized concept relating to the concept of reincarnation. In the Hindu application of the term, it applies to an endless, unbreakable chain of rewards and retribution. For all practical purposes, this chains man to the wheel of rebirth.

In light of the Pattern, a more appropriate expression for karma is energy debt and energy surplus; an equation of balance that operates in the value system of Spiritual gain. In the Pattern, life is viewed as a force. It is composed of a particular aspect of energy, moving from one point to another. There is no valuation for "good" and "bad." There is very little judgment for our actions. Instead, there is more of an understanding of the weaknesses and problems that affect us in the physical realm as we move—life after life—towards the creative ideal.

A cosmic view of reality is an actual grasp of the relationship between each dimensional reality and our placement within the Pattern as an evolving species. It is interesting that near-death experiences reported by survivors demonstrate no judgment as they review their lives; they themselves are their harshest critic. The life review they experience is an unfolding of the effects and impact of their thoughts and actions.

This is the very stuff that moves and guides the Pattern's thoughts and actions. Our movement is tracked by the emanations we leave behind us in the form of thoughts and actions. It is much like the vapor trail of a jet that has flown over where we stand. We see the trail but often the jet has passed beyond our view.

## PRESENT HISTORY

It is fairly certain we are not far from the mark of the last time we were here. There may be certain talents that were suppressed to create a level playing field in order to develop new ones. Detrimental or negative thought Patterns could have been suppressed to give us an opportunity to move forward. Yet, the sum total is you, and what you have done with it has probably reinforced what you did with it before.

We are Core Essence with a body—not a body with a Core Essence. The body is there for a period and will eventually be insufficient for your next step. Don't be too impressed or disappointed with it. There is a good chance you selected it for a specific purpose. As a Self you have the same access to the Creative Intelligence as anyone else. However, if you have not taken the time to use your potential, it's probable that your current package was selected with your help by the guides in the Pattern—a decision based on the upcoming (this life) opportunity.

Your present history—your life to this date—is of very little significance to the future you of this lifetime, even if it is interesting to you. The thought that you can change yourself at any moment is true. The force or energy you bring to any decision for change is sufficient to set that change into motion. Therefore, what you have done up to now is not as important as what you will do from now on.

## IMPACT OF ATTITUDES

Probably the greatest asset or detriment to personal growth is attitude. Attitude colors and shades every decision, action, and thought. Attitude directs our expression of reality on a personal and group basis. It is the wellspring of emotion from which we express our lives. All the emotional colorations come from attitude: hate, love, contempt, admiration, joy, sadness, triumph, failure, courage, cowardice.

Attitude is the framework, the platform from which we express our Self. Attitude will destroy or ennoble your life, and it is pretty much the same, time after time. The energy represented by attitude is seen in the individual as striations of colors. All colors correspond to the power and density of the emotion behind the attitude. Hate is seen as a deep, dark red, while thoughts of creativity are seen in pale yellow.

## INTENT

As attitude colors all expressions of energy, intent gives all actions and thoughts direction. The source of intent is thought. The more focused your thoughts are in any given area, the more readily you express intent in a solid, material way. Intent is the stuff legends are made from. All great or outstanding men and women have had the ability to express their intent in the Pattern.

Intent is a declaration, an exclamation of who you are and where you are going. It isn't the destination; it is the force and direction of what you are attempting to achieve. Realized intent puts you on the level of creator in the Pattern. The Pattern managers give a lot of attention to those individuals who manifest their intent. These are the ones who are the movers and shakers on the material plane. They are carefully guided to control the effect they have on the Pattern.

Intent is not governed by morality and ethics. Rather, it is a product of focused thought. There have been as many successful evildoers in this world as saints or holy men. There actually have been more, for a person able to manifest intent is above those controls and decisions. They are the power houses for change. They are seen in the center of new things or changes in direction. They are leaders of religion, government, and business.

The perfection of the channel between Core Consciousness and man is nothing less than the realization of thought and its driving impulse, intent, into a material manifestation that conforms to the original impulse. We realize all thought eventually into material form. We see the realization of our thoughts in the form we live in, in its content and quality. We see the imperfect realization of thought in our inability to deal with the complexities of life, as well as our shortcomings in achieving self-satisfaction, self-worth, and our most basic desires.

Our impulse is to realize a harmonious creation of intent and materialization that works with the creative impulse, not against it. This is just what we do when our desires and whims become more important than the co-creation of a continuing reality that works for all men—not just our self-interests.

The intent of the Pattern is to shape man as a species into independent units of creative expression. We have been unable to survive in a single unit. We were never able to achieve unity with the Spirit because we were always taking care of ourselves.

**SHAPING SELF**

No one is able to move beyond personal fears without some trepidation and fear. To do so on our own wisdom and courage is impossible. We are not equipped with the tools required to survive in a world which is ransomed for its products and marketplaces, driven by leaders representing interest groups, or dominated by violence and fear.

The solution to self-mastery is through realizing that Self, manifesting in a material body, already has a Pattern in place that will assure our personal survival in a materialistic world. We are, in fact, already a body of self-governed individuals who have the blueprint of self-realization implanted in our subconscious minds.

We have the means and ways of self-realization already imprinted in our minds because we are all born with the opportunity of self-realization. As Spirit, we fashioned our future lives not only in selecting parents, community, lifestyle, race, political environments, and future spouses, but by devising a strategy to break free of the illusion of life.

We have intact the database of plans and information—the complete software. When we are ready, we are able to proceed to the next phase of personal evolution with confidence, with the opportunity to succeed. The fact that the majority of us do not utilize these skills and talents doesn't invalidate the opportunity; it only stresses that we are not ready. At any moment, we are able to achieve the strategy of self-realization.

It is true that this is a process: self-realization occurs in little bits. Slowly we become aware of our potential through lifetimes of effort and self-examination. That is simply a fact of life. We are unable to experience self-realization, the ideal of Self as an individual government, because we do not have access to the tools that are already inside of us.

All of these tools are there. Our great teachers tell us again and again that they are available. Our self-help mentors describe in great detail these tools, these modes of awareness, these opportunities to transform our lives from effect to self-determination.

We all have the internal technology, but we mostly don't have the access. This is because, to access these tools, we must first set aside for a moment the urge, the drive, to survive at any cost. If we are invested in a particular behavioral mode, a belief, a thought as to what is best for us, we are closed down to the spontaneity needed, the extra energy required to break through the obstacles to self-realization. We cannot experience personal transformation if we have very little attention available to do so.

## ATTUNEMENT

When man becomes effective in governing Self, he does so by an attunement to the laws of the Pattern, which are based on creative growth. The Pattern is creative. It has no morals, ethics, rights, or wrongs. It does have a recognition that allows intelligent life to creatively grow, if that life conforms to a creative urge which makes space for self-awareness.

It will fail if it is consistently immersed in principles of self-survival. The Pattern knows that the intelligence must make mistakes to learn, without judgment, the right and wrong of a thing. This is because the Self cannot learn without developing a system of contrasts that allows it to formulate a value system—a set of rules.

The rules that work best are the rules that allow it to survive, then allow it to grow. The principle of creative growth demands that a species be more than a survival machine since there is no growth in survival. There is adaptation but there is no growth. The dynamics of creative growth insist on a marriage of pragmatism and evolution. If the surviving species develops the tools of self-annihilation, it will probably destroy itself if it is a society based on survival rather than quality of life.

By accessing the blueprint of the Pattern through attunement to the Spirit, one is given the strategy by which it is possible to work in Spirit, as well as survive. There is nothing wrong with the survival instinct. This drive has shaped our positive attributes of curiosity, expanded intelligence, and given us an inherent generosity in times of abundance. Our survival instinct is part of the Pattern's creative urge for us to move through the earlier phases of human development and onto a life in the Spirit.

## RECREATING ATTITUDES, TRANSFORMATION

The fundamental concept we learn as children is that of responding appropriately to commands and control requirements. We learn the mechanics of correct behavior, learn as much as we can, obey the rules, and understand that the things we say have consequences that reach beyond our understanding. As we grow into adulthood, the same principles pertain, yet in a much more sophisticated context because we have become more sophisticated.

Our responses to others' behavior, attitudes, and the cultural mandates of where we grew up, all take part in our attitudes. It is this conglomerate of unrelated attitudes that is the focus we bring to our adult lives. Some of it changes—the bulk remains.

Attitudes towards other's behavior form the basis of our interior values, as we are asked to respond in kind. Attitudes cover everything from self-esteem, to how to respond to unexpected circumstances. They are the color and strength of emotion. They guide our actions to the point where we respond to any circumstance with almost total automation.

That is us as robots on automatic pilot. By our mid-20s, we have formulated a set of behavior that will guide us to the end of our lives, unless modified by circumstances that have a deep emotional impact.

The unfortunate aspect of this automation is the fixed responses in which we live, encumbered with beliefs having little relationship with Spirit. This is because the nature of Spirit is fluid—a degree of flexibility that we cannot hope to achieve. Our insistence on applying control in all circumstances dampens our response to matters of the Spirit. Unlike matters of the material world that if missed can be recreated, we often lose the opportunity to change ourselves, our personal level of creativity, as Spirit passes us—seeking those who will be co-creators in its unfolding of life.

The Pattern holds no remorse for our missed opportunities. From its view, we are eternal beings and can always be approached at some later date—even though that later date might be another lifetime. Spirit demands a flexible, willing attitude to work with, to help it complete its unending task of upliftment. If we are encumbered in an attitude that isn't creative or dynamic, we are likely to miss our opportunity to move forward in personal Spiritual growth. The touch of Spirit is accompanied by signs for us to follow. However, in the density of our beliefs, we are unable to interpret the conclusions.

The call of Spirit is addressed to individuals who are at the apex of transformation from the group mind to the individual mind. The call goes out through the Pattern's managers to a specific area of influence. It is an irresistible call as Spirit seeks to replenish itself. The Pattern is indifferent to our minds and decisions. It views us only as energy potential.

As honey is to a bee, so is the touch of Spirit to the individual Self. Once touched, they are forever haunted by the experience of rightness that they felt when Spirit used them to complete a task, however small or seemingly insignificant.

We are born again, a new combination of genes and energetic potential, and still we remember the touch of Spirit. In time, we come to identify with the creative urgency of Spirit. A small fire is awakened in our Selves, and we become Sons and Daughters of Core Consciousness, representatives of the Spiritual light, an army of workers in the fields of life, bending to the task of Spirit.

These memories become the root of future experiences, however insignificant at the time. Each is intertwined with the other until there is a critical mass of experience that triggers transformation. Transformation occurs at a root level in the Self. Having experienced it, we understand forever the mystery of unity—the unity of all living things—the essential bonding of matter to matter through the free flow of energy.

Transformation is the process of raising one's energy field from one frequency to another, a speeding up of consciousness to the degree that there is a marked difference in the perception of reality from one moment to the next. As we are exalted, we experience a shift in awareness from one point of view to another. We see, feel, and literally taste the difference in frequencies. In a sense, this is the payoff of the work and faith we have held to over many lifetimes.

This peak experience, enlightenment, or cosmic consciousness was once celled the fire of the divine, holy inspiration, *samadhi*, and baptism of the Holy Ghost.

Spirit chooses the method, timing, place, and content of this transformation. It often comes suddenly at a moment that is best suited to the work of our guardians and guides in Spirit. Sometimes this arrives as a small change, a slight shifting of attitude and depth of understanding. Sometimes it is a tidal wave that stuns the mind, holding us in a suspended moment of forever. Transformation occurs outside of time as endless waves of experience roll over us. The manner and depth of the experience is very personal, yet inevitable when we seek attunement with the Spirit—and the Pattern. It is our payoff, reward, acknowledgment, sign of favor for the work and toil of self-realization.

Transformation comes to all and is unexpected; it is the right of uplifted consciousness. The experience follows a pattern that is as predictable as it is mysterious. It is the re-creation of each Soul, a step out of our past history towards growth and change. Spirit welcomes the miracle of transformation. Our attunement to the frequency of creation constructs a living bridge from the material to the spiritual.

This bridge, built over lifetimes, allows for the free access of energy from one dimension to another. It occurs in our soul-mind within the vast passageways of unused and available energy centers. Transformation thoroughly reorganizes the channels of atti-

*Chapter 9: Expressions of the Pattern* 129

tude, replacing these with an essential understanding of the Self held captive by our ego.

The ego has no part in the transformation of Self, a finer, more creative energy Frequency. The ego soon lies dormant in this process, supplanted by an identification of Self with Spirit. This greater understanding holds no place for the conceptions of limited understanding. The ego dies and is replaced with a living, vibrant sense of life and its relationship with Spirit. The creative urge cannot hold fixed images, fixed responses, or preset agreements and ideas. These are discharged as useless ballast in the shift from a fixed now to a living now.

The process of transformation to deeper potential is symbolic. The mind, as it is trained and used by the ego, deals exclusively in the realm of symbols: power, money, position, sex, security. Everything we experience is processed through myriad filters of symbols; a manageable arrangement designed to reduce the friction of consciousness when processing the trillions of bits of information experienced in a life.

As we experience transformation, our set of symbols is replaced by a new set; this is much like the process of upgrading the language of a computer from one level of sophistication to another.

Our new set of symbols allows us to experience, to realize—for the first time—the nature of our movement into a greater reality. These realizations are the bonding of all parts of awareness with each other into a coherent whole. We see the parts and pieces now of who we are here in this life. As this shift occurs, we experience the totality of all that is, realizing that separation is illusion—a fixed bit of legerdemain contrived by the ego to unify our endless images of past lives. We see the process of replacing the ego with its counterpart of Spirit and realize that ego is insufficient for the job of integrating this new reality.

Like the computer analogy, when we replace one operating

system for the other, there is no going back to the old version. It just won't work anymore to recreate and live within a previous consciousness.

The Pattern is dynamic. It rapidly shifts its essence. We often cannot sense the new experience in the old paradigm. It's useless to backpedal. That is literally why we cannot go back to a quieter, more peaceful time. We go forward, ready or not, caught up in the drama of transformation.

# CHAPTER 10:
# UPLIFT

*In its intricate functioning, the Pattern is an awareness of a gradual, relentless process of change and modification.*

### TRANSFORMED CONSCIOUSNESS IS A NEW PATTERN

Our lives and being will be recreated into a new level of consciousness, into a new Pattern of Being. All forms of consciousness experience and express this as an integrated personality, geared to the full potential of Self. Man to date has been fixed into the old paradigm of survival. The new paradigm is survival in cooperation with the Universal Mind. The effect of transformation is the loosening of the symbol of the older mental constructs in favor of the more fluid, creative ego, managed by the enlightened Self.

The characteristic of the new enlightened self is appropriate to the goals of Spirit. There is no investment in continuing the old version of Self because it does not accommodate the newer, expanded version of reality. This newer expression of consciousness brings the human species to a state of being that is a physical and mental derivative of the older paradigm of survival. Spiritual transformation is often viewed as mental/Spiritual change—an expansion of our perceptual capabilities. We see the shift in mind as expanded awareness. A shift in consciousness also corresponds

to physical transformation.
We are all heading towards transformation. It is inevitable. All forms of consciousness experience uplift into a higher level of consciousness. All pieces of transformation unlock the potential of the Universal Mind to express itself in every Being. Transformation, individual and as a group, may occur at any moment. All we need is an activating agent.

## 2021: SOLDIER'S RETRIEVAL

We walked a while, then I asked my Guide to check on our next retrieval location. Little did I know I would be retrieving myself in the past.

She pointed to a softly glowing light. Eventually we arrived and I found our retrieval, who was one of my past incarnations of consciousness, a Frenchman, a soldier, a Chevalier, fierce, proud, and royal. As Google says: Chevalier, (French: "horseman"), is a French title originally equivalent to the English knight.

I was fighting to stop the English invasion of France during the Hundred Years War. I saw a horseman engaged in a fierce, bloody battle, fighting off the invading army. This was the Battle of Agincourt, a site located near the city of Azincourt, northern France, that took place in the realm of created reality known here as the realm of Modern Illusions (common names include *maya* in Hindi, and *bardo* in Tibetan) on October 1415 (Saint Crispin's Day).

I had found one of my lives there, a soldier who had been killed on the battlefield. He was a horseman and when his horse stuck in the thick mud, he had been torn from his saddle by a long leaf-shaped spear with forged hooks. After he fell, he stood up and engaged in sword fighting, cutting and thrusting. He battled on, defending his comrades, when a spear took him in the throat and cut through the neck, severing muscle, ligaments, veins. He died in minutes.

I walked to him, my past self, and was upset thinking of him fighting endlessly on that field to defend an army defeated hundreds of years ago. He died, then fought, then died again. I stood next to him and watched the battle for a while, seeing the terror and pain. I had seen movies about this fight. This was more gruesome: severed heads, bodies punctured by spears, arms and legs lopped off by swords as their heavy armor weighed them down in the mud. Men dying and choking in mud and blood, screaming for mothers, wives, children, their God.

At first he ignored me, then as I continued to stand next to him, he stepped away from his fight. I clearly did not fit here. Only he could see me. Everyone else ignored me as they engaged in this slaughter. Weapons did not touch me. That seemed strange to him.

He walked up to me and asked me who I was. I said, "I am here to bring you to heaven." That got his attention. I suggested he stop fighting for a while and come with me. He looked at me and was now terribly upset. He said, "I am in a serious fight here. Why should I leave?" I pointed to the ground, to a very dead man whose beautiful armor was covered in mud and blood. His throat was torn open. Blood drenched through his armor and garments. I said, "That is you." He did not believe it. He was not dead; he had been fighting just a few minutes ago.

I suggested he look closely at the man's face and engraved armor insignia. He did that. It was his. I said, "You died here; would you like to see a priest now?" He looked down again and nodded. A very practical man. We walked out of the melee as he watched his comrades being endlessly slaughtered on the field, horses screaming, dying men calling out. Together we traveled to the City of Lights for him to meet his fellows in Light.

I was badly shaken from this experience. The sounds, the smell, the screams unnerved me, though I have seen the end results of the physical body many times. I have never become used to these experiences.

**REMEMBERING**

The Pattern is the very design of our reality; it is the heartbeat of the Self. It is the creative flow of evolution manifesting as all forms of matter with its shifting consciousness inextricably woven into every aspect of our lives, the integrating intelligence that provides balance and direction in the process of our Spiritual upliftment.

The concept of a driving creative force is neither unique nor new to man's diverse cultures. Every culture expresses concepts of the inexpressible, struggling to describe and picture man's destiny. This is often described as an uncontrollable force that needs to be seduced and wooed with courage.

Man expresses the unknowable in large concepts, Gods, Guardians, and Powers, yet often does not build a personal relationship with his Creator.

The Pattern always existed and always will exist as a dynamic Creative Intelligence operating outside of our perceptual range. Outside of the constraints of time and space, it exists as a theoretical dimension of alternate reality. Yet, it interweaves with our reality.

Expressing the Pattern as consciousness is a description that allows us to experience it. The creative, intelligent force's purpose is to uplift consciousness to a new form of evolution.

We move forward now, faster and faster, passing through each level of conscious reality in a ceaseless march to the Creator, where, ultimately, we stand as co-creators of the Pattern itself: its caretakers, managers, planners, and directors. We are partners in Creation and authors of the myriad realities in which sentience now swims.

Eventually, in our refined capacity of multi-dimensional Spiritual awareness, we experience an identification or merging with the Pattern. This occurs as small illuminative experiences where we recognize the underlying oneness of all forms of matter.

This unfolding awareness of the workings of the Pattern takes place over lifetimes; multiple existences in which we are subject to the directives of our teacher—physical reality. We can't shake it, deny it, or misplace it. Our actions come back to us time and time again. It is a fruitless struggle to fight off the approach of supersensible awareness. It's pointless. In its intricate and mysterious functioning (at least to us), the Pattern manipulates us towards this awareness through a gradual, though relentless process of change and modification.

We are test subjects experiencing varieties of consciousness to perfect our awareness of ourselves.

Imagine yourself as a personality living in the form of either man or woman, with experiences spanning thousands of years, unaware that you are living and dying to be born again and again. In each lifetime, you pick up an essential piece of wisdom, a nugget of priceless experience, slowly polished under the grindstone of reality to a brilliant luster.

Imagine awakening to the workings of the Pattern gradually, wary of change. Either way, we gradually open up to the potential of our lives.

**DREAMS AND INTUITION**

Our awareness of the Pattern comes through dreams, then filters through the levels of our consciousness as intuition, foresight, and psychic awareness.

Dreams are where the unconscious mind dramatizes our emotions and provides guidance and counsel. Yet, they are also the active interface between Spirit and man. What we are unable or unwilling to grasp or discuss in our waking hours becomes an open dialogue in the dream state.

The unconscious mind is the gateway to the alternate dimensions of reality that coexist with us every day. Our Core Essence, or the Spirit Self, or Self, directs the flow of information and drama that we experience each night. This flow-control mechanism is "the dreamer," which sets priorities in the nightly drama we experience.

Not all dreams are guided by the dreamer. Many of our dreams are feedback loops of repressed emotions. Some are nonsense dreams caused by certain foods, or illness, or the position we sleep in. The dreams composed by the dreamer are intelligent. They use the available symbols stored in our minds from birth, mixing these with attitudes towards individuals, groups, and objects. The point of this nightly drama is to educate us and move us forward in the design of the Pattern.

The beginning of comprehension is a grasp of concepts, internal discipline, and education. The more we grasp and understand about our reality, including our own perceptions, the closer we come to understanding the nature of reality. As Werner Ehrhardt, of EST Seminars, aptly expressed, "Understanding is the booby prize of life; direct experience is its reward."

Core Essence encounters frustration in introducing us to new ideas and concepts since we are constantly matching our thoughts and inspirations with the existing order—and structure of our mind. We filter all experiences to such an extent that the most effective way to move past these barriers to understanding is a direct shot of an actual experience of whatever it is the dreamer is trying to tell us.

Upon completing the data transfer from the Spirit into our unconscious mind, each dreamer sits back and waits for the full effect of our choices. If the recipient of this data is a key component of the Pattern (remember the value of an energy component), and the information isn't wholly assimilated, the data will be available in our next life. Use who you are! Embrace the blending of information and direction with the unconscious mind will in turn integrate all aspects of our conscious mind.

Intuition is our conscious gateway to the Spirit, and ultimately the Pattern. It's through this higher form of inspiration and guidance that we create the linkage necessary for direct communication to the Creative Intelligence that guides and manages the Pattern.

These descriptions, while enriching us as they develop perceptual road maps, hinder us in the unconscious drive we experience to be reunited with the Pattern. There are no descriptions, other than pejorative ones, for the rich fields ready to be harvested in the intuitive relationship between the conscious and unconscious mind.

We live and die with an astonishing plenitude of personal resources. We continue to wonder what it is that we are experiencing when we close our eyes every night. The expanding rich interplay between our unconscious mind and the dreamer holds its own rewards in creativity and fullness of expression—a possible doorway to alternate realities.

The dreamer beckons and we either follow or don't. The dreamer neither cares, nor is interested in what we do. Eventually, we all rise and climb from our perceptual boxes, growing wings of light, and fly from our nests into the ever-expanding reality of Spirit.

## WORK WITHIN THE PATTERN'S STRUCTURE

As beings existing within the Pattern, we are free to act and live within the boundaries set by our personal- and group-energy debts/surpluses. As Spiritual beings we are free to go where we please, believe what we choose, and live as we please. That defines an ideal world.

As energy configurations existing in multi-dimensional realities within the Pattern, our location becomes part of a complex formula that is heavily skewed by past lives and future objectives. We are pretty much born into the location by our greater Self's choice.

We live and die within proximity to the location where we are born. This conforms with the needs of the Pattern as it exerts a managing influence over the workings of our energy debts and, overall, our evolution as a species. We work and toil in the location that accounts for the predetermined placement of our energy configuration within the Pattern. Prior to being born, we choose, or are assisted to choose the location that suits the unfolding of our new personalities.

The composition of the ideal location is its energy net (the influence of energy sources). It includes your mineral/chemical composition, geopolitical influences, economic forecasts for the duration of your life, the location of those who are an integral component of your life, and the growth opportunities available during the period of your life. In a sense, all of these are calculated to produce the best opportunity for your particular setting.

People working with the Pattern push consciousness forward. That is its job. The agreements are made before birth. Bodies, intellectual and emotional capacities, family, location, and personal destinies are preselected to achieve the greatest impact possible for the mission we accepted before birth.

So, where we live does have a value and meaning to the Pattern's managers. It does affect the outcome of the Pattern on mostly a local level. Sometimes though, through the combination of intent and goals, we achieve great things and affect all people and things. These are people who, through unbending intent, approach life and its circumstances without reason—or what we usually consider reason to be.

## GRACE AND THE LAW

As the Pattern moves through our lives, we become enmeshed in its laws. The law of energy balance has the most impact. We are awakened to the Pattern, contrary to the demands of balance as a function of grace. As defined in Christian theology, grace is the forgiveness of our sins by the Holy Spirit, and it is in this context that its workings are explained here.

Cause and effect are the movers of our world. They are the basis of the law and cannot be diverted or subjugated by external physical forces. Once enmeshed in the world, you are here for the ride until balance is once again achieved. What then allows us to move past the rigidity of the law? The answer is grace: the working in our lives of the Pattern as it signals a return to Spirit. We didn't come to this place and time by accident.

Our presence was selected with great care from the beginning of our creation as a Self. Because of its nature, it is suited as a test site for our emerging Spiritual skills. These take time, and a location where there are no tricks or mirrors to evaluate their validity. That place is here on earth, in the form of consciousness. All of us are working from the same general frequency. We are therefore subject to the same laws, the same cause and effect, rules, and codes. Exceptions don't violate the rule. There is universal agreement in symbols, extending from dreams to near-death experiences.

Here we are, survivors of lifetime after lifetime, familiar in large part with what to expect and how to behave while we are here. Yet, we are seemingly unable to change our basic attitudes and motivations. What will knock us out of this catch-22 that seemingly keeps us locked into reality at the same mundane pace, life after life? Grace. Where does it come from? Ironically, the Pattern itself uses the action of grace, or forgiveness, without apparent reason, as a saving urge to help break us out of the loop of debt and repayment.

The Creative Intelligence didn't lure us here to keep us enmeshed in this reality forever. We came here as the result of our actions and decisions to learn and accelerate the repayment of energy we accrued in other lives. As a conservator of energy, the Pattern assesses the leverage point where Grace will most benefit our progress.

As a force, Grace pays up on our debts, freeing our Selves to pursue the next step of growth—the awareness of Higher Self. It's that simple, in action at least. Yet, it is extraordinarily complex because we are the last to forgive ourselves of our debts. We are old hands at sin and vice. We have gained considerable experience throughout our lives and have seen its impact firsthand. We know we aren't worthy of forgiveness. We know there's a lot left unsaid to others. The fact is that enough of us are sufficiently moral to think that it isn't really possible to experience absolute forgiveness.

Grace flows from self-forgiveness. If we don't believe we have earned it, there's no way we will give this gift to ourselves. The pilgrimage is a unique human expression of the need to find self-forgiveness through trial and misery. So, once a year, millions of people, in some form or another, enact the ritual of the pilgrimage to alleviate the burden of self-accusation: the visit to Mecca, the Stations of the Cross, fasting, self-flagellation, and other forms of self-accusation. We even kill ourselves if the burden becomes too great. We can't help it; we are human and see no other outlet for our guilt. Prayer is too docile a form of self-forgiveness. Guilt created in action seems to need an active expiation.

The energy-efficient Pattern recognizes that those sentient, self-aware beings called humans need a little help from time to time, or they verge on getting totally stuck in self-hate, self-pity, and guilt. At the point when the burden, or stress, of lifetimes of guilt becomes disabling, the Creative Mind recognizes that forgiveness is its prerogative. It does this when we are ready. It is an interesting paradox, that as we flounder in guilt and self-pity, we become inexorably sensitized and attuned to the sufferings of others.

We are so mired in our need to extract payment for our sins, both those of commission and omission, that, when we are ready, grace—or the balancing of debt—occurs in dramatic and fundamental ways. We are forgiven on a self-aware level where change is explicit to all aspects of our nature. The change wrought by self-forgiveness is so profound that it is known to estrange people from their previously solid relationships.

Through grace and its Spiritual impact on our hearts and minds, we become attuned to the Pattern and its workings. We no longer see life as a fixed destiny but view life as a form of co-creation where we are participants and not victims—where the Spirit listens as we pray. Our attitudes change when we are engaged with life: not standing back and taking it for granted or seeing it as something to be endured for the sake of our children.

As the Grace of Spirit transforms our lives, we see the fullness of our decisions and the futility of protecting ourselves and our interest. Oppression is our liberator. The petty tyrant in our lives (if we are blessed with one) lifts us from pain and suffering to liberation. We are forced to know ourselves, to become our vast potential. We are capable of achieving comfort in an uncomfortable life.

Those blessed in grace are people who know to the core of their souls that they listen only to Spirit. They are a force of quiet certainty and unspoken strength. They are the bulwark of our society, quietly healing the sick, comforting the helpless, giving relief in practical ways to those in need, or those overwhelmed by the tragedy of their lives.

In these days of turmoil and global annihilation, with the

threat of evil making rapid inroads at all levels of society, the Pattern is quietly activating its own legions of saints. Saints in the ordinary sense: people putting their love of the Creator on the line for those in need. This process is gaining speed and momentum because the days are coming when the evil in men will no longer be tolerated.

# CHAPTER 11:
# PERSONAL TRANSFORMATION

*Transformation is the process of becoming
one with the Universal Mind.*

### ACCESSING TRANSFORMATION

Transformation is a process embedded within our genetic structure: the billion-bit piece of software encoding found embedded in our DNA. We are the foretelling of evolution, found in the dreams of our predecessors. We are the memory of the new proto-man who experiences life through multiple dimensions. We intentionally access the blueprint of transformation every time we turn our internal attention to Higher Self, storing bits of Spiritual knowledge as we contact a higher reality. We are like sponges that soak up reality first through the ego, then through the Self as it steps beyond the process of self-identification, to Soul-identification.

The Self is an aware aspect of Spirit that manifests self-awareness through the body—gaining experience and wisdom. It is true that not all of us care to turn our intellect inwards and experience Self as an aspect of divinity. At this moment, it isn't required of all people. Newer Selves, which are those entities experiencing life for the first dozen material experiences, are more interested generally in ego gratification because their priority is to experience; physical reality is immensely gratifying. It is easy to become lost in the physical reality because complete identification with the material world, combined with the vitality and sex drive of youth, is overpowering.

The drive to transform Self from a material to Spiritual orientation is hidden within the ego. It won't become a factor in change until the Self has had enough of the sense world and begins to wonder about the rest of the possibilities in life. This shift is a shift in consciousness. It is a forward movement that is accompanied by a great deal of anguish because the Self's habits of self-gratification are fixed in the Patterns of behavior brought forward from one life to the next.

Life's larger obstacles to self-realization—attitudes, intent, goals, and past history—are the same obstacles we face in the transition from the ego-driven personality to the Spiritually driven Self. At this point, we are tired of the material world. There is a lack in luster, a questioning of values and goals, the results of our efforts, now and in a Spiritual sense. There is dissatisfaction. Yet, there is an avoidance of the pain and discomfort required to make the shift from the material to the Spiritual.

Transformation as a species is triggered by the Pattern, as it sees the shifting in balances between peoples and cultures. The Pattern is the best gauge of the need to move from a material to Spiritual base, or from one step in species evolution to the next. We really don't have a clue as to what the next evolution of man will look like, because embedded in our genetic code is the prototypical man of the next level in Homo sapiens. We would never point to Neanderthal man and express our close affection for their intelligence, organizational skills, or ability to manipulate opposing digits.

Proto-man, or the next evolution of man, will feel much the same way about us—a nostalgic affection for his ancestors and not much more. Change will occur slowly and pass almost unnoticed by man's contemporary peer group. That change is occurring is evident; the how and when isn't.

## TRIGGERING EVENTS

The triggering events of transformation are affected by a combination of Self-maturity (the mastery of the physical, mental, and emotional in past experiences) and the realization that survival isn't contingent upon personal effort. The transformative experience occurs when the individual has turned attention from the survival self to the Spiritual self. It is a cumulative process of self-recognition that occurs within the Self. It prompts the personality to recognize the availability of energy to assist in the internalization of inward-seeking Self-expression—the union between Spirit and Self.

The matrix of change is in the availability of personal energy, and the discipline of personality as it seeks to respond to this internal prompting. Our awareness that we are being urged to change—to radicalize our approach to self-survival to the extent that we are unconcerned by death—can be either strong, a series of illuminating experiences, or fully integrated so that we do not even realize we are undergoing the change affecting the foundations of our consensus reality.

Our transformation is a very personal matter for it affects our very being in a fundamental manner that can never be altered or shifted. There is no going back to the use of before. We don't want to, though our memory and racial penchant for nostalgia will periodically force us to do so. We are fixed in consciousness upon this transformation until we begin again the process of moving from one set of constructs to another.

The Pattern's view of the transformative process is not personal in nature. Energy recognizes energy, and sees it as an opportunity to forward its agenda—that is the realization of the creative intent. That we benefit is almost incidental; the Pattern realizes this and creates for us more sophisticated realities to experience. It isn't uncommon for the transformed individual to move, or feel the urge to get away, to go somewhere and think the whole thing through.

### INDIVIDUAL TRANSFORMATION

People aren't prepared to accept the possibility of mass transformation, thinking instead that it occurs singly. Events that have been triggered by cultural changes, as well as demands upon the Pattern to effect large-scale energy shifts that conform to the creative intent, shift us as a group from the group-governed Self to the self-governed Self. We will see transformation on a personal level on a massive scale. This sense of change is more than a change in calendar dates to a new millennium; it is a new state of consciousness that impacts every fundamental value we hold.

We don't need to see transformation from the perspective of Spirit to understand that these changes are occurring. Each moment is a flight into new levels of consciousness. We understand immediately that we have irrevocably changed our perceptions of reality.

The event of transformation in an individual has no precedent or internal reference point. As the process implies, it is a fundamental change from one thing to another, a shift in a change in consciousness. It is the minimal use of energy by the construct of the Pattern, a new personalized Spiritual reality, maximizing the energy output of a single source of self-aware consciousness. Over lifetimes of experiences we wait for that exact moment when the experience will benefit most the evolving personality.

## MARKERS OF TRANSFORMATIVE EXPERIENCES

The Spiritual transformative experience occurs finally in the realm of consciousness, impacting all levels of our energetic bodies, allowing us to access reality in a way previously unknown. The shift in awareness causes the realignment in working symbols that allows us to experience what was always there, the immense intricacies of spirit reality, the moment of Now, an expanded potential of being.

Outside of the causal relationship we have cultivated with time, we are able to see ourselves as a self-occupying body, as a fragment of consciousness differentiated from the greater consciousness that we all possess, when we are not perceiving and living life within the material of flesh. We are hampered in experiencing the unified nature of life because we are unable to access its full reality through the vehicle—the body—at this moment in our evolution.

Transformation is the process of becoming one with the Universal Mind. It isn't a stopping point, or end. Nothing fits that description as life is ongoing in a multitude of forms and expressions. Transformation is important to us because it gives us the tools, and personal power to use those tools. The result of many ages of discipline and dedicated self-research, the event marks the opening of the Self to a stronger, more dynamic relationship with Higher Self. It is wholly a personal event. It isn't triggered by other people, teachers, mentors, or Spiritual leaders.

The event is the fruition of effort; a reward. We are the inheritors of our birthright in assuming consciousness. Beneficiaries of a deeply personal change of worldview that conforms to no other experience of any one Soul. You are a unique expression of Spirit, and there is no one like you. You are irreplaceable in the fit of the Pattern. As this event unfolds in your life it does so only to you, outside of anyone's real or claimed jurisdiction.

Each experience is unique; They are exclusively yours. The expanded Self will express these characteristics uniquely as an integrated whole and as a natural outpouring of Spirit. It is an irrevocable change in perception.

The positive integration of the transformative events occurs in the realm of faith where one must accept, in patience, the variety of experiences that occurs over many lives. It does take patience to add to our existing lives, and greater patience to integrate them into our Total Self.

The nature of the personal transformation is neither benign nor dangerous. It simply is, with no explanation. It's as though the Universal Mind is saying, "Since you have worked so hard to understand how life works, here are some answers. If you make it all work, we'll be back with some more." The conversation is definitely one-sided; we are given the gift, what we do with it is our job or problem, as you see it.

The expanded personality is able to survive easily, upon integrating the transformative experience. This is so even when the transformation is in apparent conflict with the consensus reality. The expanded personality is more creative, and stronger than a group that must continually check its fellow members for approval and direction.

The experience of transformation gives the recipient access to phenomenal skills that are natural outgrowths of the self-aware entity. Of course, the key component is the ultimate awareness that we are interconnected to members of the species; we share common symbols and interpretive experiences on an unconscious level that strive in time to make themselves known to our conscious mind.

This access to the full potential of Self puts the transformed personality in a position to act appropriately, or in alignment with the creative intent, naturally, and with full understanding either unconsciously or consciously.

Compare, examine, analyze, and regard conflicting views as the norm for all men. This is not evidence of inherent instability, it is a process of questioning the source and origin of ourselves. We know from observation that the winner of battle and conflict writes their own histories. We are the legacy of the fruit of triumph—of survival.

Reach for truth and grasp what is readily available. We do not realize that truth is available within the collective unconscious, the reservoir of all experience. We seek and are given what is on the shelf, on the television, or playing on the radio. We miss the opportunity to access the fountainhead of Spiritual creativity.

Step back and see yourselves as a member of a greater reality, experiencing life as individual components linked to each other by a common energy. Life is a series of moments individually accessible, increments of time carrying the potential to be changed and recreated. We have an awareness of being both here and now, occurring in this place and elsewhere at the same moment of now.

Access information from the energy of events that have and will occur, as we step outside of our time continuum into the timelessness of the Universal Mind. We are all a part of the transformed human, the proto being dreamed of and prayed for by visionaries, by the victims of life, the lost and hopeful, and by us.

# CHAPTER 12:
# AFTER AWAKENING, BALANCE

*A shift from the old to new consciousness demands our complete attention to who we are in Spirit.*

### AWAKENING FROM A DREAM

Awakening comes in its own time, without notice or fanfare. It in turn alters the view we have of our reality, our family, friends, the workings of our society. It forever alters the manner in which we deal with everything from eating breakfast to praying. This alteration is the opening up of our awareness, the expansion of our scope of possibilities and alternatives.

Opening ourselves to more than an improved intuition we see patterns of behavior where before there was just movement. Trends are perceived where there was once random action as we become available to the Pattern, co-creators of our reality, no longer limited by our society.

Through the mystery of linkage, the Pattern impresses directly upon our minds the flow and ebb of its movement in our affairs.

We expand then to a global view of man as an emerging sentient species in the universe, The gateway has been opened and it is our choice to act as is appropriate to our personal needs.

Our gift is choice. Use it.

## UPON AWAKENING TO THE PATTERN

The Pattern seeks balance. It is a natural law that acts with or without our consent. Think of an infinite tunnel that curves and returns to its origin. Spirit to life to Spirit. The drive to seek balance, to conform with the law of return, is the driving force within the Pattern and so affects all its occupants.

The transition point in human evolution is the borderline between natural awareness and self-awareness, between looking inward to looking outward. The instinct to look out and see who we are marks us forever.

*We access the blueprint of transformation by storing bit by bit what is needed to contact higher realties.*

Our lives are a paradox of events that flips reasoning from logic to intuition. Left brain dominance shares functionality with the right brain intuitive process. The Spiritual, the creative intent of the Universal Mind, knocks constantly on our door of self-awareness—waiting for us, patiently, with love.

Life is a series of moments individually accessible, increments of time carrying the potential to be changed and recreated, occurring in this place and elsewhere at the same moment of now. We access information from the energy of events that have and will occur when we step outside of our time continuum into the timelessness of the Universal Mind.

### THE ART OF CONTACT

*Our minds are overloaded with information that we have not been taught to thoroughly assimilate. We redistribute these in a way that is useful to us.*

## BE STILL

The Pattern operates without the need to conform to consensus reality because it is essentially a machine, a vast network that is the result of intelligent guidance. Mechanistic in nature, there is no affecting the Pattern by prayer, wishes, or demands. A better vantage is that one can access the Pattern by attuning our awareness to its movement in both the observable and unobservable realities. This is made manifest by visualizing the Pattern's structure as a symbolic representation of energy forces.

The closest we can come to understanding this multi-dimensional structure and its basic force is achieved by attuning to its intent. This attunement is achieved by the realization of an abstract conceptualization—the Pattern as a force, and as a movement of energy that is fluid, dynamic, and creative. The Pattern can be seen symbolically, through the subconscious mind, in meditation and in other forms of inspirational insights.

Attuning to the Creative Mind is most readily available through the quieting of the conscious mind. This is how we let the unconscious mind interpret and visualize the shape and content of the Pattern in universal or cultural symbols. It is the natural inclination of the Pattern's managers to assist us in achieving greater awareness of their work. This gives us access to a definition of the Pattern's form.

We are accustomed to the idea that our reality is a result of the divine. We are comfortable with a personalized abstraction of creation—it suits our objectives in prayer and meditation. Culturally, there is no linkage in our mind between our view of the universe and our notion of a personalized Core Consciousness. We have no descriptions with which to fill the void between us and Core Consciousness. The early New Testament writers took time to describe angelic hierarchies with divine intermediaries. Yet we persist in visualizing that our prayers reach out into the heavens, *somewhere, some place*; we wait for a response, or some echo acknowledging our personalized consideration our specific requests.

The Pattern is the *explanation* of Core Consciousness in the sense that it is the creator of the Creative Mind's intent, in the many levels or dimensions of reality it works in. If we attempt to understand the mechanism that drives the Pattern, we will fail. This is because the Pattern is devoid of personality or self-awareness. Trying to interface with it is like trying to communicate with a machine or converse with a computer. There will be no response other than that which has been programmed into the machine, to answer select questions. The answers are structured to conform to the input; they are not the answers of a self-aware entity.

When you pray, you may well ask, "Where does my prayer go, if not to the ear of Core Consciousness?" When you beseech or make requests to a greater power, to the archetypal father, is there a destination or location where you are heard? Is there a place where the intent of the request is received and processed? Your prayer does go to the ear of Core Consciousness, the divine aspect of you. Your Self is the interpreter of your desire and translates it into creative intent through the workings of the Pattern.

You pray, your Self listens. It passes the energy of your intent through the local area manager (angel) into the network of the Pattern, where it is processed. The response is a description of intent from the universal managers, the archangels of the Pattern who are responsible for the working of the Pattern in our section of the galaxy.

The response is integrated into the Pattern as an energy variable. It is then plugged into the mechanics of the Pattern as potential to be used by the local area manager directly. In exceptional requests, the response is returned directly as a response matching the need of the sender, if it has been impelled by the focused intent of the sender. People who have mastered the realization of thought into energized intent—a form of powerful prayer—shorten the response time to their requests or directed prayer. They are more likely to realize a response from the Pattern's managers because they have learned that thought, the origin of prayer, can be very powerful. It is at its most powerful when uncluttered by self-doubt or the disbelief in the effectiveness of asking for something from unseen entities.

Transitioning in consciousness from point to point literally takes no time because the process does not, in fact, occur in time. The process of prayer and its answering energy occurs outside our dimensional framework and in the creative construct of the Pattern. There is no beginning and end to the request or the prayer. It has all happened, is happening, and will happen simultaneously. This is the basis of understanding: Core Consciousness knows your heart before you pray.

No request or thought is unheard because everything has been heard since the beginning of time. Our whole shifting reality, a path that occasionally seems almost tortuous to us, in fact has no complexity at all in the mind of the Creative Intelligence. There is no mystery, for all mysteries are known and understood. Their outcome is clear to the Creative Mind.

*It is good, practical advice to be still and listen to the small still voice within, to cut off the constant chatter of the ego as it strives to gain dominance over our Selves. We will never be able to transcend the mental clutter of our minds until we quiet down our constant stream of thoughts and begin to listen to the responses that our prayers create.*

It is the condition of our culture that we are bombarded with massive amounts of information, data through visual and aural stimulation. Our minds are overloaded with information that we have not been taught to assimilate or redistribute in a way that is useful to us. We hear, but we do not understand what we hear.

It actually takes personal "downtime" to assimilate all of this information we receive. Is it any wonder then that we pray loudly and quickly? We fear being embarrassed by someone observing our prayer, and we think that our friends will ridicule us or call us unsophisticated.

How can we begin to model a form of effective, provocative prayer when we can't even reconcile bowing our heads in respect to our Creator, asking for help in our lives? Prayer is a focused, streamlined request from us, our combined ego/mind, the force that impels the universe to act. We ask Core Consciousness to intercede. On a practical level, we deal with Core Consciousness's mandated hierarchy, the angels, or what we call managers.

We request without clarity and so it's no surprise that we receive mixed responses. Yet, more importantly, *we ask and do not wholly believe that our prayers are answerable*; we secretly think they are too difficult or unusual to merit response. The fact is that the Creative Mind listens to everything we think, to all our prayers, understands every motivation, as well as the source of our prayer requests even before they are spoken.

The problem is that Core Consciousness in His wisdom has structured the Pattern to respond to our requests to the degree that we drive the request with focused intent. We pray, we receive. That is the law that has been mandated by Core Consciousness.

We need to understand that the clarity of our prayer—the degree of its focused intent and the clearness of our request—is the impelling force that drives our prayers. Without this, everything falls short of its mark. The Pattern responds to the force of intent and nothing else. Our divinity lies in our experience and ability to create clear prayer, as well as the degree to which we have faith that our prayers will be answered.

Faith drives the power of prayer, for it impels the energy of prayer directly to the Creative Mind. Without certainty that our prayers will be answered, without certainty that there is a creative force, without certainty that miracles are possible, we force ourselves to wait. We wait for our prayers to be answered; that is all we do. Without the underpinning realization that there is a greater force in our lives assigned to the task of guiding and protecting us, we stand naked in the movement of force through matter. We are perpetually overwhelmed by the turmoil of greater minds, buffeted by the strength of their returned prayers.

Remember that prayer is a tool. It is the open line of communication between us and Core Consciousness. There is no regard for right or wrong, or how and who uses the tool. All of us—from the best to the worst—are entitled to use the power of prayer for whatever it is we think we need, for whatever distress we experience. There are no judgments or liens against the user if they are, in our judgment, a "bad" person.

Core Consciousness reserves the right to judge us, and frowns upon our judging others. This is because we don't have the knowledge or clear sight to assess and judge their motivations, hardships, or reasons for what they do. Remember that the victor writes history to suit their version of reality, and all of us have been taught the righteousness of our way of life.

So, we pray, each of us, in our own way. We demand, request, argue, whine to that force or being that best represents our conception of Core Consciousness. We are confident we have a clearer picture of who that designated receiver of our prayers might be. We are not deterred that the person next to us might be talking to someone very different.

The prayer line doesn't care to whom we think we are praying. What matters is the force and energy we put behind our prayer—the clarity of intent that we issue forth behind our prayers. Life is a level playing field when you consider that all of us have the same equipment and the same opportunities. Most find it very discouraging that apparently unworthy people, even those destined to live a Creator-less life, have their prayers answered. There seems to be little justice or wisdom in the manner we are apparently rewarded.

Often, we quit trying, thinking our prayers are wasted. We do not understand that we are defeating ourselves even before we begin. We are an impatient society, expecting immediate results. We think that we are special in the eyes of Core Consciousness, forgetting that all are loved. We know in our hearts that we are worthy. Yet, we do not spend time polishing our hearts to the brightness of a diamond. We are confident that others in apparently less fortunate circumstances than ours—the handicapped, homeless, ugly, or fat—are somehow not worthy of the attention of a loving father.

We misunderstand the reality of Spirit. We are perceived by Spirit not for our wealth, our good looks, our humor, or our successes. Instead, we are viewed as *a focus of energy*, a place, or position in reality that is the confluence of mind, Spirit, and clarity of expression. It is true that evil diminishes the human Spirit, but most of us are not evil. Rather, we are usually simply involved with our self-interests to the exclusion of all else. We do not see ourselves as an accumulation of focused energy, a gateway to Spirit. We see only our bodies, our position in life, and our apparent successes.

We fail to realize that we are much more.

We are the accumulation of all experiences, of past acts of goodness to others, of our determination to experience the essence of Spirit. We are the sum total of our Spirituality. We cannot see or believe because we do not listen to Spirit as it attempts to override our minds and speak directly to our hearts. We touch but do not feel. And so, discouraged and alone, we pass by our Creator-given opportunities and wait eternally for the miracles we have been promised will materialize. We do not understand that we are living in the greatest miracle of all, the promise of Core Consciousness to live in our hearts. This promise was made to us before life—the promise to let us stand as co-creator with the Creator in the unfolding of our Spirit.

## LISTEN: MARCH 29, 2022 TO JUNE 1, 2022: RETRIEVAL WORK IN UKRAINE, TAGGING ENERGY BODIES

Early in the morning I shifted consciousness to Ukraine to see if there was a need for assisted retrieval work. The target was a city block of residences that had been leveled by artillery shelling. The city was Mariupol.

I moved in and through the ruins of the recently demolished buildings, ignoring fires and heavy smoke. There were dozens of souls shocked into place by a transition that was fast and brutal. There was no preparation for their sudden deaths.

There were people both trapped inside the demolished building and dead. I saw the dead people were tethered to the building, unable to accept their transition. I pulled out many of them from deep in the building. Their essential energy bodies could be seen and felt. These I turned over to my fellow crew member, who shifted them to the Death Ring for repair, rest, and preparation for transit to the City of Lights in continuation of their journey, whatever that was.

I found a smoking cloud or ethereal particles in one location, drifting in the fresh rubble. There was no form or visible essence. I did not know what this was until, by searching and then focusing on the core energy body, I saw a woman, mid-80s, who while in her apartment had been hit by an artillery shell and instantly vaporized.

I could not grasp or touch her energy body. It ran through my fingers like fine sand. I could barely see it. Puzzled by this situation, I remembered a past-life experience of my own when I had been vaporized by an explosion of uncontrolled energy in Atlantis, as a Priest Scientist. The re-assembling of quark-like particles took centuries. My energy body had to be reframed and then the ethereal body restructured. There had been no retrieval, no reclamation. This had to be done by my higher Self, a hard lesson that could be used here. How to proceed?

Go back in time! Tag her energy particles before her death.

I rolled back my consciousness two days before her death, and visited and "tagged" her essential energy core so I could retrieve her destroyed energy body by retrieving her energy signature. Smoke or no smoke, the permanence of the essential self can be identified if there are energy tags.

I moved my consciousness back to my "now" position, there in the rubble, and reached out to touch the tags. This worked! Slowly I captured her essential core energy body, tag by tag, until I held her in my hands. Then I shifted myself to the Healing Center and handed her to the Healers who were ready to start their work.

The hard work of Spirit becomes easier as time passes. There are no schools or workplaces to prepare us, no materials made available to pull the work of Spirit off. Where do we see a sign that asks us to meditate for 10 minutes a day? How many times have our priests and rabbis asked us to pray and meditate on the nature of the Spirit, of Core Consciousness? We nod our heads, then go home and watch television or call friends to come over.

We may be a culture lost in misplaced Spiritual values but don't worry. The majority of the planet is with you. We have no effective means to effect change on a fundamental level other than prayer and counseling, exercises that take time.

So, when you pray, understand that the largest obstacle between you and Spirit is *your mind*. The receptors may seem like they are not working, but they are only temporarily out of order, disrupted by a little static interference from our belief systems. All is not lost—not at all—for the final trump card of the Spirit is grace, the redeeming touch of Spirit that can unplug the pipeline.

Prayer and meditation will activate grace and clear the channel between us and the Creative Mind. Persist, take the time, refuse to be swayed by the internal mental suggestion that prayer and meditation are reserved for the fey, or the unsophisticated.

The process of Spiritual dialogue is an enrichment that transcends the cultural mandate to conform, the scientific mandate to align ourselves to proofs and conditions. The only thing that stands between us and a Spiritually enriched life are the beliefs we hold about the value and rewards of the Spiritual life.

We don't consider the possibility that a Spiritual life adds to our value, our ability to do business, our relationships with family members, neighbors, and co-workers. We only see internal pictures of crazed old men in orange robes, white tangled beards, or old ladies hunched over crystal balls. We see from our picture of reality, not from reality.

Real life isn't demented, distorted, or unhinged. Real life is the wedding of Spirit to mind. Every day we see only the fruit of the mind, in abuse, violence, and other excesses. Rejoice in the simplicity of a dialogue with Spirit. Reap the rewards of contact—experience the guidance that will smooth your life and give you the strength to persist, even in events and circumstances that would normally leave you weakened and befuddled.

Your relationship with Spirit is *your* business, no one else's. Ironically, your Spiritual Self holds you accountable for the Spiritual quality of your life with a degree of ferocity that the Spirit itself would never deal out. It's a mistake to think that your only reward is found in heaven. You are living it; right here, right now. We are much tougher on ourselves than any avenging angel could dream of being.

# CHAPTER 13:
# CONTACT

*The ego is not interested in growth, it is only interested in a static position that enhances its power.*

As you begin the process of clearing out the pipeline between you and your Spirit, you begin to see the absolute integration of Spirit in the everyday world. The once-perceived nuttiness of the Spiritually inclined begins to appear as an ordered, logical progression in life, from the ego-driven to the Self-driven. In the process of life itself, we begin to clear our mind of the values and ideas placed there by our teachers. Gradually, our obstructed inner child begins to heal and mature. Eventually, the day comes when we can express who we are, not who we think we are.

As you focus on the Spiritual world, you see that there is no "there" and "here." There is only the all-inclusive Self that moves freely in all places and locations. The strong identification of ego with place is replaced by the Self, and its relationship to Spirit. It's a gradual shift from one paradigm to another; from living within our mental pictures of what's *so*, also known as reality, and what *is*, a greater reality.

With self-evaluation and a commitment to listening for the response of the Spirit to our internal dialogue, our mind actually becomes more ordered and spontaneous. Strictures of thinking are only induced by a rigid set of beliefs that we acquire over time. As the mystery lifts and we see that there is no mystery, we become integrated with the expression of Spirit as it seeks to guide us in the balance of the Pattern.

Contact with Spirit is an increasing volume of inspiration from our Spiritual Selves to our Physical Self. As we become grounded in Spiritual reality, our inner ear, our vision, becomes clearer. We experience greater possibilities inherent in a Spiritual relationship with Core Consciousness. By becoming unbound in doctrine and beliefs, we are available to the living experience of Spiritual reality. Our lives, once cloaked and shrouded in guilt and fear, become enlivened with the revitalizing energy of a fluid, working relationship—the energies that power life.

As the doors of perception open, so do our options. Our view is expanded from one level to another. With a slow integration of the physical and Spiritual, we stay grounded in a working reality while moving forward in life. Our potential is increased as our limits are decreased—all attributable to our ability to listen to, to feel, and to see the reality of the Spiritual life. This process of integration and opening is not debilitating, nor does it make us prey to others.

**TAKING ACTION**

As you become empowered in Spirit, you have the availability of additional options unhindered by fear. Individually we move beyond the controlling influences of power and doctrine. Thus, we are freed to experience Spirit intimately and with a precision once unavailable to us. We hear and can act with integrity and power.

The picture of the suffering martyr, murdered in the name of a Spiritual cause, is a popular vision of what happens to people who oppose the power structures that control our lives. It is an indictment against those even thinking of making a commitment to the Spirit. Once, the very nature of the martyr was to rebel with cause against the conforming doctrines imposed by religions and governments. It is an enfeebling picture that defeats our experience. Yet, those who died in Spiritual resolve were freed from fear. They were the exception, for those living in Spirit are rarely the victims of life. Instead, they are the ones who empower others in the experience of Spirit.

It is a historical precedent that those who experience the clear vision of Spirit are revered for their wisdom. They are not rebels.

In the light of Spirit, we are all one. We are born on the same planet, and our divisions are only momentary deviations from the balance of the Pattern. The Spiritually enlightened have no fear because they have experienced the wholeness of life in every aspect of their lives. Through a separation of fact from fancy, they experience the path to greater Spiritual reality and become immersed in its healing energy.

*Life without Spirit is a condensed, dark, action-packed drama without reference, satisfaction, or depth. It is subject to every whim and circumstance, every bully, every controlling personality or would-be dictator.*

We are taught to respect religion from childhood. From young adulthood we are taught to question and doubt the real truths of a Spiritual life. By adulthood we are confused, perplexed, and unable to reconcile the varying messages we receive from the pragmatists and dreamers that populate our mindscape.

Turn your picture of what a Spiritual life is 180° away from the materialism of *proofs*. Trust in your inner sense of rightness and truth, and you will begin to see the real values of life.

We are eternal, here only for this brief span of time. We are limited in a body that soon dies from wear and tear. We are condemned to limited perception of a reality that "sees" only a portion of what it senses. We are structured to accept only a portion of the divine aspect of Self that resides in us.

*Yet still, we are the inheritors of Spirit.* All of our Holy Books verify this truth. Science is now beginning to question the basic precepts it held so dearly—astonishingly, the demand for proofs is gradually being satisfied. We find it is only our limited view of self-potential that obstructs our growth and keeps us diminished. We are unable to grow beyond the attitudes we learned as children: the doubts, and fears accumulated through years of impressionable growth, conforming to peer pressure, unable or unwilling to question even one iota of our notions and conceptions about life.

## SEPARATING FACT FROM FICTION

The Pattern is verifiable in the experience of Spirit as a limitless expanding consciousness. It is the hand tool of the Creative Mind as it seeks to express its intent through the medium of life and self-awareness found in developing species on this planet and in other realities.

The experience of the Pattern is linked to the experience of Spirit, something that eyes cannot see, ears cannot hear, and, though you strive to touch it, has no substance to grasp. The experience of Spirit is available only to the inner eye, the mind attuned to an expanded consciousness of greater realities. It is important to note that that we use the word greater not in the sense of a hierarchy of life but as a *wider* vision of life that encompasses a universe of potential, a view of an unstructured universe seen and felt first in the heart, then in the mind.

You can still your mind and heart and meditate upon the vastness of the universe. You can talk to sensitives and psychics and see our hidden Self being slowly unveiled. You can use tarot, I Ching, dice, and bones, scry with crystals until the portions of your life once unseen are clear. And yet, even having done all that, you may never experience the ineffable network of the Pattern.

The Pattern is the hand of Core Consciousness, an angelic hierarchy, a physicist's dream, the archetypal matrix, the foundation of creation. It is seen in the subtle, gossamer movement of events, in the inexorable drama of karma, and the saving measure of grace.

The Pattern has been with man since he took the first plunge from Spirit into material manifestation, from a sexless, Spiritual identity into the grounding polarity of materialism. Do you see electricity or high frequency sounds? Are the creations of your thoughts describable? Can you go beyond the event horizon or through black holes into new realities? Not yet, not now, but all will be achievable within the new human consciousness. We experience little of life beyond our five senses at this moment, mostly because we don't believe there is more to see.

The Pattern is not the stuff of life. Rather, it is the stuff of creation and so resides beyond mere events in the realm of *causation*—the birth of first principles. We need to differentiate between phenomena in order to experience the root of cause, unburden our senses from the dynamics of life, depart the structured universe into the formless, unstructured cosmos. Can we as humans go past our notions of what life is? What we are capable of? Can we move beyond expectation and allow ourselves to see without prejudice or fear?

We may know the root calculations of the world, we may create new life through gene recombinants, or we may extend our lives by rejuvenating the genes that say we are old or young. Still, having done all this, we may never see past the barrier of materialism to allow our finest instrument—our consciousness—to grasp the intangible, to touch the Spiritual ether with faith and intent.

Buried in the effect of action and thought, we see only the four dimensions of reality. By suspending beliefs, we are able for a moment to directly experience the force of Spirit as it intertwines with our lives. In that moment, we will see ourselves as greater than mere power and strength, greater than our thoughts of grandeur and exploitation. In that moment, we will experience the real world of mind touching its source.

The facts are clear. We are here, today, living in the reality we have conceived from our desires and thoughts. Every hour of every day reconfirms that our thoughts are our reality. We may not remember all our thoughts and desires, but are confident that somewhere, somewhen, we decided that this is the best we can achieve. Our minds say that this is fact, and that other experiences of mind and Spirit are fiction.

We declare to the world that we are real, and we are. We operate as efficiently as possible in this frequency of materialization, complaining sometimes because of a discomfort or an injustice. We don't strive to change. We accept, and live, and die. That is real, or so our minds proclaim and our egos demand. There is nothing else to see or believe in. There may be a Core Consciousness. If so, I'll pray and hedge my bets. If it's true, I'll come out a little ahead. Or better yet, I'll live life in the form of devotion, dedicated to a life that hedges all bets, that reflects my beliefs, my parent's beliefs, a comfortable life that cleaves to the precepts of religion.

That is our life, as either agnostics, believers, or occupiers of the vast middle ground of doubt and unknowing. We find acceptance and contentment, having done the best we could in a demanding, uncertain world where, at any moment, our lives can end, be destroyed in the vast, unknowable mechanism of fate.

Unfortunately, what we do not confront is this: we have only just begun to understand the paradox of life, and that which we have held as fiction is fact—the fact that life is Spirit, that Self is mind, and that we exist through time in timelessness. We are all creative potential... but, we ask, for what?

Hold on to your reality, your beliefs, your precious conceptions, your life without cause and effect, or Spiritual responsibilities. As people approach a greater scientific understanding of life, we approach a greater Spiritual understanding of life and its place in the unfolding universe.

## FREE WILL

*Co-creators, partners, and allies—we become all of these as we move from self-interest to self-awareness.*

Without hope, and in the knowledge that we are very powerful in our ability to manipulate reality, our mind is in a constant process of building the content of our thoughts. Powerlessness in the face of tragedy, as well as domination, are states of mind that can be influenced and changed through direct thought, by the act of will.

What power we all hold within our grasp to change our lives by the force of will! What power we have to find the right words to express our outrage! What courage to live in conviction of our beliefs! We are a step away from the power of the Pattern, a step away from realizing that our true oppressor is ourselves. We constantly defeat our own dreams and ambitions by giving up under pressure, reinforcing our belief that we aren't good enough, or worthy enough—that some intrinsic piece of our integrity is missing.

Free will is a key component when using the Pattern. It enables us to free ourselves of domination by others, to express our self-truths, to break the shackles of government and religious oppression—both their fundamental belief in our submission, and their inability to empower us individually or as a group. Existing in the light of Spirit, man needs no big brother or father. He is whole and complete in Spirit in a way that is untrue if he stands as a material man, defined by his foibles and faults.

We have the opportunity at any moment to transform our

realities from hopelessness and helplessness to empowerment and vitality. Nowhere in the teachings of the world's wise men, saints, and Spiritual teachers does it say, "You are unworthy." Our inspirational doctrines speak again and again of our potential and inherent strengths—and our ability to be transformed and healed at any moment.

*The ego is not interested in growth. It is only interested in a static position that enhances its power.*

The Pattern is lost in the realm of ego because it doesn't belong with ego. The two are like oil and water; they cannot even reside as neighbors. As the Self gains wisdom and experience, and becomes more attuned to the working of the Pattern, the ego puts up a greater resistance to this threat. Self is a threat to ego because it is the eventual exterminator of ego.

There is no place for unreformed ego in a Spiritual life because the ego wants to live forever and is not interested in the finality of death. Spirit knows that there is no death and is uninterested in self-aggrandizement because it is plugged into the vibrancy and energy of the Higher Self. What cannot die is not interested in death. Spirit sees death as illusion and actually spurs us to diminish our egos so that, in the long run, we are able to experience undiminished Spirit's power.

## TODAY'S DECISIONS, TOMORROW'S DESTINY

Today's decisions, expressed from the insight of creative expression, are those that form tomorrow's reality. It isn't surprising that the most radical and far-reaching changes are now seen in ideas and concepts put forth by their creators as written or visual symbols. This is intensified by our reluctance to experience change—an alteration of what we are comfortable with. Our basic intolerance for change only allows the submission of ideas for review, consideration, and debate—i.e., an incremental but never wholesale change.

By nature, we change in small steps, by pieces and parts. There are no giant steps for mankind, only baby steps that one day materialize as change—a change that had been coming well before the event. The Pattern urges us to transform our lives, our attitudes, and our self-view, and it does this in keeping with our nature, slowly and in incremental steps, with a push or a shove maybe, but never a cataclysm.

Every major event in our personal separate histories is traced to a volume of ideas and actions that lead to change. We are changed in continuing phases of material incarnations. Like a bottle we fill ourselves increment by increment with experience.

Through our ongoing need for a changing environment and for a shift in material form to prevent depression, boredom, and ennui, we move gradually towards transformation. We size up then reconfigure our beings to allow the energy needed for transformation.

Change *appears* to be quick, because, before an idea's time has arrived and reached fruition, there is no visible change. We can see the winds of change, but we cannot affect its progress or direction unless it becomes a natural evolution of a workable idea.

We demand change, transformation, the experience of Spirit. We become disheartened and diminished when nothing occurs. We spurn our own dreams because they didn't happen. The truth is that our demands were not ignored, nor were our dreams subjected to derision and ridicule. They simply did not happen on our personal timetable. They were not invalid—unless they were unreachable, unless they were unworkable. We don't really know the true effects of our desires and dreams because we don't see the results of the energy that we put into them.

It is alien to our concept of reality to plan for an idea that may take generations to come to fruition, an idea that may take generations to be realized. Still, it is the rare idea that is realized immediately. Every creative concept has been manifested upon the foundation stone of someone else's thinking.

The fact is every creative concept really takes lifetimes to achieve.

Unfortunately, we are taught to expect immediate results, and to value our efforts on these results. We are only too willing to set timetables and goals for self-determined projects before they are even remotely achievable.

## CHAPTER 14:
## THE PATTERN UNFOLDS SLOWLY, LIFE TO LIFE

*Spirit knows the results of our efforts: we have all won the game, captured the prize, merged in Spirit, and have left this world forever.*

Through prayer and meditation the Pattern unfolds slowly, with deliberation and intent. We can see its unfolding, either clearly or through a haze. This is our reassurance, the answer to our prayers, the clear indication of our existence in the complexities of life. We see the will of Core Consciousness—the creative intent in the Pattern—and we find assurance and solace for the seemingly absurd, ironic happenstances of reality.

We see the eventual fruit of our ideas and actions in the unfolding of the Pattern's creative urge. We see that *time is the essence of change*. There are no emergencies that were not foreseeable, no risks that are not secured in foreknowledge. Yet, we see none of this because we never really expected our prayers and wishes to be answered.

We walk through life forever with the hearts of children. We are denied our potential. This is because, like children, we demand instant, measurable gratification in all actions and thoughts. "Otherwise, forget it," we say. "The effort isn't worth it." Then, we stumble onto the next event in our lives.

We don't settle for *potential*. Instead, we settle for results and cut ourselves off from life in the Spirit. We denounce our Total Self (our Total Over Soul is the group of souls within which we are created or belong to through preferred associations) as ineffectual bumblers. We do not realize that, like nature, the creative will unfold at its own pace in order to answer our prayers and demands. It does this in its own time, with a measure of compassion that surpasses pity. The Pattern works to build our growth in the perspective of eternity, a degree of loving ruthlessness that is neither cloying nor stroking. However, it is not necessarily comforting, as we demand from our earthly institutions and religions the assurance that all things will conform to the comforting structures described within their proscribed canons and laws. We find comfort in form, denying content. We find assurance in belief. We outlaw Spiritual experience from our lives.

**CHOICE AND THE CO-CREATOR**

We are what we believe and deny of the creative reality of Spirit. That is how our minds work, how our emotions flow. That is who we are as a people. It is only by commitment to a supernal reality that we are able to transcend who we are and discover the truth of our source—the living, dynamic Spirit of Core Consciousness. This is man's natural evolution from the material to the Spiritual; each phase of this reality is natural and without judgment. Neither is greater or lesser than the other.

There is no judgment or evaluation of the rightness of this, except for what is true in our own hearts and experiences. When making the transition from the material to the Spiritual, we are our own judge and jury, passing sentences and convictions upon ourselves for our thoughts and actions.

We choose the sentence and the conviction—it is not chosen by our Spiritual elders and mentors. We are our most ferocious judges. In time, we decide to return and repeat the experience to gain from the wisdom we acquired in failing and succeeding wherever we were last. We recreate the same experiences, give ourselves the same opportunities, and face the same frustrations and failures in the hope that we will succeed where before we failed. From the view of Spirit, there is no time limit, end game, or final decision. There is only *now*, the forever of opportunity to learn and grow.

Spirit knows the results of our efforts. We have all won the game, captured the prize, have merged in Spirit, and have left this world forever. We have won our many battles already, in sometime when, someplace where. All striving, worry, concern for dominance is a wasted effort. These are not particularly reassuring words, given our fears, doubts, and worries. Yet maybe this is the golden ring of eternal life we all seek, our experience of being backed up against the wall, then succeeding finally in the face of defeat and despair. Accepting the counsel and input of Spirit has not yet been considered.

We can choose daily to live our lives as a reaction to the circumstances and events we face, or as co-creators in the progressive evolution of Spirit as it seeks to move us forward in life to Spiritual perfection. The suggestion that we are co-creators can open the doors of awareness to the expanded potential of infinite choice, infinite reality; a creative, responsible, affirmative action that supports all of creation, not just our little segment.

As co-creators we contribute to life, and do not detract from life. We grow and recycle our efforts in perpetual motion. We determine and choose, hooking into the vibrancy and dynamic urge of the creative word. We select, then act in support of life, and we see the results of our actions echoing outwards, resonating in tune with the sound of Spirit entering into life.

Co-creators, partners, and allies, we become all of these as we move from self-interest to self-awareness.

## The Gifts of Spirit in Transformed Man

*In the transformative process, we actualize new awareness by awakening to the reality of underlying energy structures.*

**TIME AND TRANSFORMATION**

We say that time is experienced, one moment to the next. Our futures are always tomorrow, our pasts are yesterday's memories. We know time, and we divide it into smaller increments, giving it a value that we do not accord any other dimension of reality. We do not know time, however, as *a moment of now*, described then passed, always moving forward.

The fourth dimension of our reality is time. It is a measurement we all agree with, therefore we have created it as a mechanical standard. We forget that time is a function of the physical world and occurs *exclusively* in this physical world. Time occurs in our perception as an exaggeration of reality. It is slow, fast, coincidental with reality. It is always occurring in our perception in a manner that corresponds to *our* thoughts, *our* emotions, and *our* interpretation—of both internal and external stimuli.

We are taught the workings of time as children. We have no natural grasp of its function, are spatially sensitive and time oriented. We learn about time as we mature and understand that events appear to unfold in a linear fashion. They do, and so we assign value to time's increments. We set our perceptual clock to these values, working to create a synchronization between the increments of time and our interior sense of being.

Time as a dimension of human reality is unquestioned. The perception of time occurs so fluidly that we don't experience it as anything but an external event that is linked to all eternal events. In the transformative process, we actualize new awareness by awakening to the reality of underlying energy structures. We see (and sense) depth, breadth, width, and time. We integrate these with the perception of spatial relationships from multiple, interpreted views—not from one location, but from many.

This shift of perception in the transformed Self will dispel the fixed view of life as four dimensions of unvarying reality, as seen from the front view of a single person. Rather, we will perceive that time is an experience of depth, contrast, and perspective that is subject to change at any moment within a cohesive, dynamic reality that expresses unity in every phase.

We are sensitized to the variables of energy as we break up conceptions ingrained from childhood. When we view ourselves as self-aware beings, we break the ironbound linkage we have with outmoded conceptions. We see ourselves as Spiritual beings. It is a process of refocusing our view from one position to another.

This view is dazzling because it is much more real. It is more intense in its unfoldment and potential than the almost flat scenery of the senses we experience every day of our lives. By "expanding," we become attuned to potential and realize from the framework of Spirit that we are capable of sensing and seeing more than the energies we have become acclimated to. We are better receiver sets because we know in the process of transformation that we are not bound to a single point of view; we are all points of view. Our sensory organs are freed to sense more than what our culture tells us is real.

There are no rigid natural laws demanding that we synchronize internal and external events. We do this for convenience, as well as for building consensus agreements with others, to arrive at an agreeable interpretation of what has occurred. If we break our bondage to the consensus agreement, we find that our internal sense perception, married to the perceptions of the unfettered mind, are actually more accurate than what we see with our eyes. We call this facility *intuition*, though we usually attribute intuition to a compilation of nonverbal cues that we analyze for connections and trends.

## NOVEMBER 30, 2021:
## MERGING WITH UNCREATED ENERGY

I finally stayed at home tonight, resting and pushing off the demands of sleep after a visit where I as usual merged with the constant flow of uncreated energy. This mutual give and take strengthens my core energy and is, plainly stated, a sensual experience as much as a rejuvenation within my energetic body. Unlike uncreated energy, created energy is a result of focused intention wrapped in the manifestation of your desire.

Uncreated energy is the flow of unmanifested energy, the black luminous fabric of this earth and its surrounding rings. Uncreated energy is the key ingredient that shapes the Pattern of human consciousness, a holographic energy grid that structures our consensus of what time and space is.

Every being on earth embraced and agreed to the restrictions and rules of time. Beings who exist outside of time live in an endless Now that is unaffected by the entropy of aging. Life on earth, unlike energetic beings, is deeply affected by the shifting sands of time/space.

Here we are planted until the congruence of all of the disparate realities we exist in signals a movement away from physicality to energetic bodies. Great news in the long sight! Regardless of the endless diminishment of the body, we as a group move on. This is ultimate uplift as created by the founding group who designed and created earth.

Created energy is the realization of intent through the manifestation of its chosen expressions: actions, Spirit's gifts, our life structures, simple wishes of wealth and love. All of these are preceded by the shaping and push into reality of intent. Each of us creates intent, utilizing the availability of the uncreated energies in this universe (others are significantly different). Manifesting intent is our reality.

Our reality as defined by the intent of the creators is framed within time and space. We are what we think and emote. No surprises in that known fact. When life changes are needed, remember that we create our reality. Imperfect creation will be painful.

On returning from my experiences, I rested, pushed the chair seat back, and fell into a perfect balance of borderline sleep and active awareness. This sleep/awareness is a very active state and a precursor to the release of the soul into infinity.

And that is what happened. With a shock my consciousness shot out from me into a circular shape, ringed in a kaleidoscope of colors and rotating white light. It was like a pulsing starburst. I was there in a flash of no time and then reached out to touch the ringed lights. Instead of entering as I wanted to, my energetic body/soul was forcefully pushed back into my physical body.

Completely focused on this new experience, I formed the intention to go back to the pulsing rings of color and light. I very much wanted to go there and see what this was. I knew that somewhere within the rings were answers to my many questions. Again, I was pushed back into my body. Consciousness was flicking back and forth with clarity and speed. I thought this must be a dream. I had never had (or did not remember having) this experience before.

It wasn't a dream. My back ached from resting too long in one posture. The tingling continued throughout my body.

Again, I looked to that place and thought I could go there but I was not allowed to stay. I saw clearly now with my eyes the pulsing ring as though through a telescope.

At this rejection I felt a strong push of emotion and desire. My life's credo has always been, "Move forward to face the unknown. Never quit."

Some part of me insisted the rings were there for a reason. For me. A gift? A Trojan horse? I couldn't back away.

My consciousness again on direction moved out from my body. I could see both my body and the shaped intent of my energetic body. Focused on reaching out "there" again, I collected my consciousness and for a third time shot out of the room into the heart of the rings. I entered and, in that fraction of a second, saw everything and understood nothing.

I was snapped back into my body like an elastic cord returning to its source.

Three attempts were enough for now. Tired I closed the connection and decided to sleep. And I did. I fell into a dreamless state of darkness and rest.

As powerful as this experience was, I still do not know what happened.

The Pattern is all this and more. Through a process of closing down external stimuli, we can open ourselves to the internal perceptions we experience every moment of our lives, and generally disregard as useless and distracting information. As a result of the transformative process, we gain natural access to this internal awareness, as well as the ability to receive sense impressions internally from any source, anywhere, anytime.

As we see the underlying reality of nature, we break the sense bondage, the chains to visual interpretation we are forced to live with. As a result, we become comfortable with the sensory input we once discarded. Our expanded ability includes seeing what the nature of our reality is. It is not the mere reflection of light striking objects in space, or the optical illusions we often mistake for Spiritual phenomena.

Through patience and exercise, the personality becomes able to access the new reality introduced, then enhanced, by the transformative process. These faculties include a broad range of phenomena: real experiences that cover all areas of the five senses, as well as new combinations of each. Perceptions and experiences are keyed to personality types. Each singular "I" will express a single enhanced talent of "knowing" by the demands for the balance and use of energy by the Pattern. Past experiences as well as current attitudes probably play a significant determining role in which attribute of the transformed personality is brought into use.

As the personality grows and begins to experience successive changes in perception (transformative experiences affecting the reality constructs currently in place), we add to our insights, and intuitive faculties. In addition, we grasp the availability of skills from past-life experiences. This process of growth, of change from a limited dimension, an expanded dimension and may occur over a period of years. It is more likely to occur over a period of lives.

We are finely tuned identities that are forever growing and evolving our consciousness. Through experience and a mastery of skills, we slowly integrate into self-aware beings whose capabilities are essentially limitless. It is inappropriate to measure a child's capabilities against that of a young adult, or the youth's to the mature adult's. Each, through the span of our many lives, gains wisdom and compassion, and learns to access the skills that are often overlooked in Life by younger Souls.

This same analogy is applicable to the Self: it incarnates throughout many lives, concentrating on acquiring a skill, an attitude, a talent; each adds to the whole personality. Past-life memories aren't desirable in an immature Self because the influence of a dramatic, traumatic, or key life event can sway the personality into forms of behavior that are difficult to change.

*The Self gains throughout time, for there is no permanent death as we are taught to believe. Rather, there is only process, process, process. We are dynamic in nature, versatile in creation, and utterly indestructible in Spirit. We come back for more, rest-*

*ing when needed.*

Many of us are here for the experience of life, to live emotions and thoughts in a world where creation is a matter of self-realization. Our outcasts may be here to redeem a debt, balance a character flaw, contribute to a loved one, or compensate for lives filled with vanity, pride, or arrogance.

We never really know why we are doing what we are or doing, never know why we are living life as we do. We must accept that we are initially limited in our potential because we are directed by the Pattern in expressing Self in the material world. However, growth is a given because we express the intent of the creator as certainly as we breathe air.

There is no way to know the finite details of evolving Self. That knowledge is cloaked from even the most Spiritually informed eyes.

**EXPERIENCING THE DYNAMICS OF THE MOMENT**

There is available to each of us the moment of time we know as "now." This is not the abstract concepts of past and future, but the creative, loose-ended perception of *present non-time* that occurs at the moment we perceive, yet before we remember, categorize, and file for reference.

This moment of "now" carries with it the full body of the potential of the future. It gives every action a weight and a significance that we do not relate to in the moment, but only later.

The moment of "now" is a moment of creation. It sets the direction, pace, and content for all future, consecutive moments that build our realities. The usual method for understanding the value of these strings of moments is through memory, Here, we wade through the masses of data that our brains have collected and select an abbreviated shorthand expression of what occurred "at that moment," i.e. earlier. Because we are not trained to think and remember in moments, these are usually strings of moments that occur in seconds or minutes. Our memory of them is really a lengthy remembrance; not the true memory of what we were thinking and feeling.

We are generally incapable of fully experiencing the moment, because intellectually we are unable to sort through exactly what occurred at that moment of "now." Instead, we rely on our interpretation of that moment for some sort of inaccurate analysis. We are imprecise, and our memories are distorted by related or peripheral data from previous moments of "now." The truth is we are unable to *accurately* recall what we were thinking and experiencing at any moment. Instead, we rely on of our memories to do the work for us.

We learn then to think in periods of time. We disregard the moment as something insignificant, or only partially important to our ability to perceive and understand what we are experiencing. We brush off the moment of "now" as a meaningless event; something that by itself is meaningless.

We don't appreciate that the moment of "now," as it is *created* by the personality, is a reflection of the Pattern. *Now is a created interpretation of the creative intent of the Universal Mind as it is expressed through the Pattern.* This moment always relates to us personally. The moment of "now" is placed in our conscious mind as a temporary marker of the Pattern, at a specific location of our being—a location that changes as needed, even as it is occurring.

We see ourselves as fixed consciousness, located through the tool of self-awareness, somewhere in a body. We don't experience the dynamics of the moment because we cannot see, feel, or hear them. "Now" occurs too swiftly for analysis or interpretation. The concept we recreate, each moment, of "Now" is, through the guidance of the Pattern, in joint effort with the power of our Self.

We are recreated in each moment, for the body has no elastic memory of form or shape in the realm of free-moving atoms. There is only the *memory* of shape, form, and content that is sparked in each moment of "now," allowing us to think sequentially and progressively. Without the master planning of the Pattern, we would literally disappear. The Pattern is the matrix of creation, as well as the ultimate reference point for the natural laws of creation.

The Bible notes that man was created in the likeness of Core Consciousness. This expresses that the Spiritual dynamics of the created being follow the creative laws as expressed in Core Consciousness's original creative intent. Our physical form is absolutely irrelevant to the concept that we were created in Core Consciousness's likeness—this holds true for us and for all other created beings. All forms of consciousness are remembered in each moment within the Pattern as a specific matrix of creativity, even though their essential Selves never change.

Creation is the expression of the Pattern's guidelines as determined by creative intent. Form is only an expression of need and requirement as it seeks self-awareness and unity with its creative source. We are not more developed or less developed than other forms of creation. We are only corresponding forms of material creation, using the best material expression at hand to achieve our mandate of reunifying with the creative source. We will ultimately change material form as needed, because our potential for growth is limited by this form. We will acquire new material expressions of creativity as our various Selves demand them. We are more flexible than we realize and know no boundaries in expression.

Every time we "die" and return to the creative source, we are refreshed, remembering our origin. We come back here to pick up where we left off, which gives us the opportunity to express material form in a new way, all towards manifesting our Spiritual Self.

*Life clearly is an opportunity, even in its worst or most degraded form. In any shape, it is a stepping stone to self-awareness and, ultimately, reunification with Core Consciousness.*

It is the uniform creation of form, remembered and expressed for us through the energetic structure of the Pattern, that forms the ultimate life matrix. The Pattern allows us to continue in life, moment to moment, without interruption, towards ultimate potential. The Pattern is consistent with natural laws because it is the fountainhead of natural law. As we die, our forms, our material creation, retain shape and form, until some exterior force alters them. Even in death, our creation is remembered and stored.

We are, on a Self-level, co-creators of our form. From the perspective of non-time, we participate on a Spiritual level with our self-creation. We are only limited by our experiences, self-knowledge, attitudes, and personal goals. We know the dynamics of the moment, changing from immutable to mutable. With a focused thought, "now" becomes a potential for change, and with mastery we are changeable. Transformed man becomes the master of the moment of "now" and sees the relationship between life and the Pattern in his early stages of evolution. Man eventually realizes that the Pattern is the source of created form, not just the guideline to its expression.

With the realization of the creative potential of each moment of "now," man is able to master the direction and content of creation. He is able to alter the force and intent of material expression so he is no longer subject to death—the final barrier to self-expression. A knowledge of the dynamics of each moment allows one to realize that the obstacles, problems, health issues, and personal fortune we experience every day are totally manipulatable. Part of our process is self-mastery. The basis of self-mastery is the knowledge that we are in a state of constant creative flux, undiminished by time and events. We are players in the creation of life, not mere spectators.

## RECOVERY WORK

First visit of the night was to City of Black Lights. There I plugged into the vibrational energy of success, abundance, and health. I have been working on PKE (psychokinetic manipulation of energy) skills. Here is the place to do that, where unmanifested energy potential is shaped and expressed in the reality of the rings.

The first of tonight's retrieval work brought me to what I thought at first was an angelic being. Stepping closer I saw a brilliant, light-filled expression of female energy. She was human in origin though she had passed through the cycle of life and death.

With a look, I sought permission to step closer to her presence. She gave a nod of acceptance. I reached out to touch her. My fingers then my hand passed through and into her core energy. I felt a vibrant energy jolt. She didn't flinch. Maybe she expected my need to personally verify her, to know if she was real, where she came from, why there was something different in her that she had not been willing to discuss.

I felt and saw then a depth no angelic being had. She was timeless, measureless, her essence confined within the shape of a woman. She was not human or angel or non-human intelligence. She was unique. She was a Guardian, a Forever being created before the rings, from inside the mind of the first creators who had already moved on to completion. This work was her training in the laws of sentient beings.

Filled to overload with the conflicts and dangers I faced, I walked to the retrieval site among the children there, touching their energy, sensing their pain, loneliness, and confusion. This was not a happy place.

Spirit said, "Stephen." Then I saw Stephen Elliot, age 7, from Biloxi, Mississippi, severely beaten by his stepmother. Traumatized over time, he had finally died, a death covered over by family members. He had severe brain damage. Spirit urged me to heal him before his entry to the healing center. I did what I could. Now his spirit glowed. Good to proceed to City of Lights healing center.

Holding Stephen's hand, I continued my walk and saw a girl. Her energy field called to me. She said her name was Zirri. I paused and she amended her name. "I am Zirri Bakkar, 8 years old, and I died in a barrel bombing in Aleppo, Syria." A building fell where she lived. She was crushed, and as her world darkened, she prayed to Allah for deliverance. Now here, the trauma fell off of her quickly. She is very bright, and aware of Spirit.

I took her hand, walked with both of them to the soul-retrieval vehicle named Razor, whose work as a smaller expression of consciousness was to transport these recovered Souls to the City of Lights. Alisa is the angelic being responsible for this work. A "captain" of the Razor, she seated each retrieval. As the energy space enclosed, the Razor folded itself inward, then winked out of sight.

For some reason I had always, from my first meeting with Alisa, trusted her to be present and thoughtful in all of her work. Though not knowing her from previous work, I would, with gratitude, place my Soul in her capable and trusting hands.

Alisa took the Razor after it was filled to City of Lights and then returned here. She was not letting me out of her sight.

## MOVING CONSCIOUSNESS TO AN UNSTRUCTURED REALITY

Transformation is a process of aligning personal reality with unstructured reality. This is not reality as we perceive it with our senses, but the reality theorized by physicists who understand that the underlying principles of creation are only partially explained by our personal cosmologies. This process of alignment occurs gradually because the personality is inculcated with thousands of working theories of reality based on cultural guidelines for behavior and "right" thinking.

Transformation nudges the evolving personality in the direction of greater reality, making way for unfettered thinking, a free unstructured view of potential as opposed to the dogmatic thinking that conforms to the midline concept of reality. This process occurs over vast spans of time. We don't teach the average child genetic theory or social/economic trends of unstable economies. We teach each child the fundamental basis of root science and proceed from there. With us so-called grown-ups, it's no different. We do not grasp and understand more than we are capable of.

The same principle of alignment applies to the personality prepared for a shift in consciousness, moving from one view of reality to a slightly modified view of the same object, encompassing new perceptions. This incremental shift in awareness, from the fixed here to the abstract soon-to-be-real moment of there, allows the personality to include more and more bits of information. Eventually, entirely new constructs energetic expression become possible.

Experiencing reality as an unstructured, dynamic process, we see that there is no *here and now*, no tomorrow and yesterday. There is only the flow of unlimited potential reality that is neither time-based nor contingent upon a linear format for explanation. In our string of personal realities, we occur simultaneously like a string of beads—one after another. There is no precedence of events or lives, for they all occur as a Möbius strip, right now. Since we are perceptually locked into what we have defined as time events, these things seem to happen one at a time. You wouldn't dare tell anyone to experience *later* in the now.

However, there can be a very small shift of emphasis from material-based to Spiritual-based reality, though they actually overlap and are congruous. Therefore, it can be said that a shift in perception from form (material) to its underlying construct (Spirit) demonstrates that we are essentially limitless beings, unfettered by events, circumstance, or location.

When viewing the same reference point from an expanded perception of continuous reality, it is apparent that there are no fixed positions in life that encompass unique awareness. Consciousness includes the perception of reality as events and locations happening simultaneously *and* in a series. It allows us to view any event that we focus our attention on, from any perspective.

This experience is similar to the shamanistic phenomena of placing the awareness of the Spirit (not the mind) in multiple locations *at the same now*. This multi-level awareness of different aspects of reality occurs in the fractured moment of the created "now." This is the heart of the Pattern. The Pattern is reconstructed in all its details in the infinite moment of "now."

By suspending ordinary reality, we move into this expanded, fractured moment of "now." You can describe, continuously at your leisure, from any vantage point, the experience that is the selected focus of awareness. This dimensional seeing occurs in literal *no time* or *out of time*. It is this manipulation of the reality between moments of "now" that gives the Self the opportunity to insert a reformed, reconstructed, or entirely new moment of "now," or reality. Operating from this expanded, or enhanced, awareness of reality, the personality has all the time it needs to experience each location from any perspective. It can adjust to its own reality by focusing the energy of creative intent through the Pattern back into material reality.

An example of utilizing this expandable moment of "now" to achieve a specific result is seen in Spiritual healing. The directing of energy by the healer is not measurable enough to appear that something is being done. However, from the expanded view or awareness of the moment, it is really the Self inserting a new, or recreated, description of reality for the patient.

The ability to see and experience life, from the underlying structure to the finished form (material reality) without apparent limitation is simply an understanding of Self. It is an understanding that there are no limitations in location or position when viewing life from the expanded view of Spirit. There is no geographical orientation of up, down, left, right from the view of primal, or Spiritual energy. There is only the view, or direction, of flow that is selected as the optimal conformance to the directed intent of the Self through the medium of the personality. The personality can view, only in cooperation with the Self. In this respect, the personality is much like a room containing an infinite number of televisions, each broadcasting a different signal, each reachable by focusing one's intent upon the desired view.

Clearly, what we consider reality is no more than a collection of firmly entrenched beliefs, held in common with friends and family. With access to the limitless potential of Spirit, we are able to experience life to a degree we did not think possible. We are more than the sum of our parts. We are everything, conveniently segmented into a personality that is manageable and maneuverable in what we call reality. Eventually, there will come the day when our full potential is unleashed in the fury of self-realization. Until then, we walk the path of self-creation and hope to achieve the pinnacle of human potential, reunification with Core Consciousness.

### LINKAGE OF LIFE

A third attribute of transformation is the awareness that we are all elements of the same energy, vibrating at different rates. This universality of awareness occurs as we are sensitized to the energy that binds reality into place. These are the energy configurations that have been described as the Pattern. The Pattern is the binding force of creative intent as expressed by the Universal Mind in its urge to become self-aware. In turn, it reflects itself to us as aspects that are urged to become self-aware.

The experience breaks apart our carefully constructed agreements of how life works and replaces them with a clearer understanding of how it *really* works. We cannot begin to understand reality without seeing firsthand this underlying relationship, something that can only be experienced in the context of the Pattern—an interlocking grid of energy lines that are the binding agent of all matter, regardless of its rate of expression.

This experience of commonality that is seen, as well as experienced, is the lift-off point from a material reality to a Spiritual-based reality. We cannot profess to know Spirit without an experience of it. Our words remain hollow descriptions of spiritual uplift until the day arrives when we experience firsthand the dynamics of structural principles, the manifestation of energy constructs locking all other random energy expressions into unifying forms.

# CHAPTER 15:
# THE NEW CONSCIOUSNESS

*We are willing to risk change because we have found the replacement tools that will make the transition from a material-base to a Spiritual-base practical, if not easy.*

We live now in the change wrought by the individual creators within our Spiritual groups who sensed the need for change. It is an alteration of style and approach to the existing order. Change isn't sourced from the competitors, the winners of the race. They are too confined; they look and act too much alike to really change anything. Change is forced by the creators, the people who say, "Enough."

They stop the process long enough to question and challenge its direction. They demand that they and their families survive intact from these changes. They are the "have nots" and the people who are not rooted in *things*, who are flexible enough to move, to voice opinions and not lose their positions, and who force, by the strength of their moral beliefs, the flow of our reality.

The creators are the power generators for change, the drivers of a coming New Age. It is the traditional battle of entrenched power structures against the creative elite. History shows clearly that the entrenched power bases will win for a period, but always eventually lose. This is because the very example of the creators penetrates the hearts of the competitors, showing them new ways and areas to compete in. Change becomes inevitable, not even dramatic.

The creators are dramatic, for they symbolize the possibility of change. They express in large images and grand gestures the potential of new ideas and forces. The competitor sees the reality and opportunity of change. He picks up the fight from the creator, making alterations, modifications, and accommodations, bringing things into focus, making them market ready.

The evolution of Spiritual consciousness is now gaining enough irrevocable force that we are engaged in a fundamental change as a group. We are willing to risk change because we have found the replacement tools that will make the transition from a material-base to a Spiritual-base practical, if not easy.

We are undermining existing structures on the basis of morality and ethics. This is our own personally evolved code of conduct, as opposed to turning over our personal power to what we perceive to be superior, more sophisticated power bases. We have rapidly evolved from monarchy, to republic, to democracy, and are in the transition towards individual self-government.

## ARMAGEDDON

Perhaps, Armageddon is not so much the devil's field day as the final conflict between beliefs, between those who give and those who take, a large, boldly painted death struggle where the winner takes all, and that winner determines our reality for the next thousand years. Where the material fights the Spiritual, a reenactment of Manichean philosophies, and an actual battle between dark and light.

It is the battle we fight in our hearts and minds every day between those who control and dominate our destinies and our belief that we are as good as they. The belief that we are Spirit, eternal, undying, and a vast accumulation of experiences and devotion.

## AS ABOVE, SO BELOW

The urge towards self-government is a mirror of the construct of the Spiritual realm, the cause or source of our material manifestation of things. The Spiritual realm is the description used here for the other dimensions of being that the mind works with in other realities, or levels of energy manifested in the Pattern. We are not the densest material form nor are we the finest. We are the mid-road to evolution in a sentient species, a materialization of thought in the form of condensed atomic structures that are most closely aligned to the creative expression of Core Consciousness.

We are the best potential for this thought. Our destiny is to realize the Creative Mind in our lives, until finally realization clears up all the obstacles between us and the Creative Mind. Then we disappear in the sense that we are absorbed in the Creative Mind as a completed identity, and our need to learn the relationship between thought and matter is completed.

As we are completed, we return to Spirit. We lose our ego identity (which we do after every life anyway), lose our desire to manifest in the material world, and take up new tasks in new realities.

This continuity of form, experience, and understanding is a realization that the urges, impulses, and actions originated within the First Cause as creative intent. They are passed along to the material plane—that is our reality—as laws and codes of behavior in the form of ethical codes and moral behavior. We act out the truth of the creative impulse through these structures. They are the imperfect manifestation of the Creative Mind. This is not unusual when the channel of expression—our mind—is an imperfect receptor; we get what we understand, in bits and pieces of realization, some of which are shaded by attitudes and temperament.

The perfection of the channel between Core Consciousness

and man is nothing less than the realization of thought and its driving impulse into a material manifestation that conforms to the original impulse. *We realize all thought eventually into material form.* We see the realization of our thoughts in the form we live in—its content and quality. We see the imperfect realization of thought in our inability to deal with the complexities of life. We are unable to achieve the most basic of desires, a continuing sense of self-satisfaction and self-worth.

Our impulse is to realize a harmonious creation of intent and materialization that works with the creative impulse. In contrast, disharmony occurs when our desires and whims become more important than the co-creation of a continuing reality that works for all men, not just our self-interests.

### INTENT OF THE PATTERN

The intent of the Pattern is to shape man as a species into independent units of creative expression. Historically, we have been unable to survive in a single man / single vote environment because we were always driven to assure our own personal survival at all costs. We were never able to achieve unity with the Spirit because we were always taking care of ourselves. The altruism of man, achieved through self-sacrifice and through determining action as demonstrated by his religious and cultural mentors, can't be sustained in the face of a diminishing sense of personal survival.

### BLUEPRINT

The blueprint that has been embedded in our Self since its creation is a sophisticated strategy to attune our minds to the creative impulse of the Pattern. This allows the Pattern to orchestrate our evolution on a personal basis, as opposed to the way it is being done now. We are now being managed as a group, as *a species*. As such, we are faced with decisions that bypass our individual needs and address the needs of the group. As a group species we are asked to make decisions that guarantee our survival. Of course, we have made it this far. We have not intended our group destruction. We have created the survival tools needed to fend off extinction.

Our personal decisions and actions will determine more clearly our future Selves, our relationship with the Universal Mind, and our own personal standing in our evolution as a species. Our radical departure from group dynamics to individual dynamics is expressed in the demand for a greater degree of accountability for the actions of our leaders. We require the enhanced ability for our decisions to make a difference in a greater compressed period of time. *We are learning quickly that the age of mass communication—instant media—frees us as individuals, and condemns of us as a group.* We can talk to and react to every situation, person, or event more directly and powerfully than ever before.

Our ability to communicate in real time as opposed to elapsed time is the first step towards communication with the Pattern. When we act in attunement to the Pattern, we are acting out our personal Self-mandate of creative growth. We are coming nearer to the process of moving from the group to the individual.

In the process of becoming better informed, of relating to our power structures, or of becoming able to develop a consensus quicker, we are moving closer to the realization that we are a self-governmental body. This is a leverage point in history where the dictates of the power groups are succumbing to the greater knowledge of their individuals. This is coupled with our ability to react as a greater group to the lies, deceits, and dirty tricks of the empowered group.

This leveraging is the beginning of greater Spiritual awareness. As time passes, more and more people will be able to make their own informed decisions. This is in opposition to the decisions they accepted from the power groups because their personal survival was at stake. The informed individual is a citizen of the world and is the master of his leaders. A Spiritual life isn't one holed up in a monastery or led from the bowels of a cave.

The era of the sanitized saint is passing; the need to hide is passing. The saint is the actualizer of man's process of dreaming reality and actualizing reality through thought. The saints and holy people no longer belong stashed away in hidden places. Rather, they belong at the forefront of the process of evolution. They are spending less time in meditation and more time in a hands-on mode of demonstrating the concept of individual government in a practical, utilitarian manner.

*Our saints were the first prototypical self-governing bodies, as individuals, because they lived attuned to the creative impulse. Through prayer and meditation, they realized that the distance between themselves and their Core Consciousness was much closer than anyone believed. They knew they had the capacity to set aside ego in favor of Spiritual Self.*

They knew reality was not in the world of survival. They knew reality was in the Creative Mind. The urge of the Pattern for upliftment was music to their ears and hearts. They saw the grand and vast working of the Spirit, traveling the Pattern's depth and breadth, perceiving regions of heaven never spoken of in common literature. They conversed with angels, understanding that the universe is a vast mystery and is unknowable to any man.

Saints became associated with the characteristics of madmen. Though sanctified by their religions, they were always held in awe, but at a comfortable distance. This was because men as a whole didn't understand the panorama of experience these people conveyed through ordinary vocabulary. Concepts of divine fire, heaven's gate, Spirits bathed in white fire, demons, and glorious heavenly voices were the words of madmen. Yet, when expressed by these mystics, they were heard with awe. They described the road that all men would travel, as well as the travails and then ultimate contentment man would experience as he entered the Spiritual land. These were not visions of the here and now, but visions of tomorrow, of some place over there.

They lived the Pattern, relying on its infinite wisdom and potential, using it as toll to converse with their Core Consciousness. The Pattern became a way of life, a threshold of limitless opportunities. It allowed them to use their earth-bound body as a receptor/translator for the input of universal truth. They accessed their personal blueprint of evolution, uncovering the potential for wisdom, truth, understanding through the Spiritual experience.

They experienced, then understood Spirit manifesting as man. They perceived the drive to perfection as expressed in his developing awareness, intellectual curiosity, and ability to love family, cultural groups, and enemies, the ability to sacrifice for others, the denial of the survival urge, the destruction of ego for the sake of giving. All these mysteries they now understood *in the context of the creative urge.* Man was really laying down the framework with which to return to Spirit, for experiencing Spirit directly through the expression of higher goals in the real world. In addition, man was accumulating enough mass to defeat his evolving inertia towards recognizing someone other than Self as a valuable recipient of a higher ideal.

We are witnessing the passage of the creative urge from above, as expressed by the Pattern, to below, into the mind of man in his daily reality. The capacity of enlightened beings for understanding the nature of man, as well as their ability to experience the truth of being not as a body but as a Self, set the stage for man's next step in evolution towards Spiritual expression without the need for an intermediary. Without this language of potential that holy men and women brought into being, we as a people would never have seen the gate to self-realization.

The experience of mind-realizing Self is increasing in all segments of our society. We are seeing the changes in pieces. Yet, when the data is collected, it argues for a broad-based transition in awareness from the strictly observable proof to the internally verifiable proof.

*The majority of us don't need a scientific belief structure to prove the reality of a Spiritual world. We know in the thousands of personal ways we experience Spirit in our lives that we live in a greater reality, whatever it may be called at that time.*

Our days of requiring massive clinical proofs are coming to a close as we satisfy ourselves that our connection to Spirit is provable. We can verify for ourselves the truths we require to know that Spirit walks hand in hand with us, every moment of our lives. (The proofs for Spiritual and psychic phenomena are established, though not yet dispersed to the point where most individuals are changing their thinking in regard to these matters.)

We are no longer able to use the question of proofs to stop inquiry or research into the phenomena related to expression of the Spirit. We are now on the threshold of being accountable for our unexamined beliefs. There is now a Spiritual revolution in human consciousness. An uplift of humans to a higher degree of consciousness is occurring right now, though it's rarely noticed.

Most are afraid to re-experience life and its relationship to Spirit. Our unwillingness to reexamine attitudes and decisions stops our spiritual growth. For many, living the beliefs instilled in us as children is fine. After all, why reopen the affirmed conclusions of childhood of 30, 40, 50 years ago?

We often think that the need to reexamine our beliefs and lifestyle is a useless venture because so little has changed since we were first introduced to the concept of Core Consciousness and the works of the indwelling Spirit.

It is unacceptable somehow to allow for the idea that, by attunement to the Spirit, we have access to every tool we need to govern ourselves, to address our deepest fears about our self-balance. The concept of transformation is as foreign to us as learning a new trade, a different language, or suddenly possessing skills beyond our aptitudes.

### THE NEW PATTERN OF CONSCIOUSNESS, UPLIFT

The characteristic of the new model is action that is appropriate to the goals of Spirit. There is no investment in continuing the old version of Self because it does not accommodate the newer, expanded version of reality. It worked for its purpose. However, it is now outmoded by a sleeker, more streamlined model of experiencing higher levels of consciousness seamlessly. This model accounts for and explains more of the mysteries of the universe than the previous model that combined superstition with primitive scientific experimentation.

*This newer model is the Pattern's shift from the old mode that described the eventual destination of the human species to a state of being that is a physical and mental derivative of the older paradigm of survival. I call this Uplift. All forms of consciousness will experience expansion and awareness as the earth itself does.*

*Spiritual transformation is seen as a mental/Spiritual change, focusing on an expansion of our perceptual capabilities. This process is more than that. It is a shift in energetic signatures as an evolving, expanded awareness. we do not realize that, as consciousness shifts, there is a corresponding physical transformation.*

### MAY 10, 2020: MEDITATION OF ENERGY

Tonight, I took a simple visit to the City of the Patterner where the flow of yet-to-be created matter is a silky, silver black light that embraces us and shifts in all matter. I knew I had to power up my energetic body to make this visit.

Moving through the layers of consciousness to arrive and merge into the City would take strength and focus. In this place there is an infinite supply of potential black energy. Creative potential that, when expressed through intention, shapes all material structures.

Black energy is a shimmering black and silver flow of unrealized creative potential powering the transition from intent to physical expression. This applies to all of the realms, from Earth to the upper reaches of hyper-consciousness. Uncreated energy is the coin of this realm. I rested, immersed in the power and beauty of the black light.

Experiencing the one-pointedness of endless moments of Now, I thought, "Here, I can stay a very long time." Then the Master of the City of Black Lights popped up in front of me, giving a polite greeting. They are all polite in the upper realms, though you must hold onto your wallet. He asked me what was needed.

I slouched a bit and said I am very, very tired. He then checked all his energetic bio-enhancements he had gifted me and said, "You're good, there is no mechanical malfunction. Go back to your reality and rest. Come back when you have passed from this life into Spirit and have processed out the human aspect of your personality. We shall make new things for these new humans."

I was humbled to speechlessness. This was an invitation I would not pass up, an invitation from the Creative Lord of all form.

As always, he seemed to frown then blinked out, leaving a sparkling light of energy, a communication trail of messages and future directions. I felt the ring he gave me and looked at the design. What was this spiral with a shining star close to its center? "There is nothing I can do here now. This is your business." Later I found that this spiral galaxy was our galaxy, the Milky Way.

As I rested there a little boy walked up to me. I looked, then looked again. I could not believe it. The boy was my son, a well-loved six-year-old. He said, "Hi, Dad, what are you doing here?"

Recovering from this surprise I said, "I'm okay, just powering up here for my next trip." He smiled. And I said to that smile, "It would be great to live long enough to see you grow up." I didn't think I would watch him grow and become a man. He returned my smile and slowly grew taller, a boy passing into manhood, moving through each phase of life. Young, middle aged, old.

Though his body gradually changed shape in age, his face maintained his rounded features, and the sincerity sparkling from his brown, piercing eyes. I then saw him as an old man kneeling on a bare wood floor in front of a burning incense stick, rocking in prayer, preparing for his death. The shrine was wrapped in candlelight, I saw family images, mine as well. "Good kid," I thought. "He remembers his father in his own end of days. His life was well-lived in Spirit."

He honored and loved his parents, knowing that he would soon join us.

I was happy, then sad, yet at peace with myself, watching him grow and become a man of integrity and honor in his commitment to a life of Spirit. I now pray that this will unfold as he showed me, knowing Spirit's decisions are never fixed.

He then reversed the aging form until once again he stood before me as a charming and very six-year-old boy. He said, "Bye, Dad, I have work to do," and left. I felt the truth of this statement stream through me like sunlight on a summer morning.

He is the next generation of shapers, creators, caretakers, and inheritors of the new Consciousness. I moved back to my body, an incredibly happy, very worried parent.

*We become more than who we believe we are. The evolution of all conscious expression on earth, from stones and rivers to all forms of life, demands this change. We are the base of a new model of consciousness, transforming the energetic structures that define who we are.*

We are all moving towards transformation. The deal is done. All the votes are in. Human consciousness will continue in new forms and expression, surviving the coming disruptions of the earth, and society, as well as in our hearts and minds. It is only a matter of time and patience before we experience this mystery of becoming Spirit in body, mind, and heart.

The premise of this shift in consciousness is a real, tangible change in perception, the ability to adapt physically to these changes, to eradicate the unwanted behaviors we live with, the behaviors that threaten our survival.

The future Pattern of man is in the present mold of man. All the pieces of our transformation are locked within us, yet accessible in a shift of consciousness that will unlock the potential of our Universal Mind.

### BEGINNINGS, ENDINGS, BEGINNINGS

How does this story end? Well, it never really ends. Each story of who we are begins, then ends, then begins again. We all progress to a fuller consciousness, heading towards our own expression of creation. We are capable of transformation at any moment. The tools are within us.

Fulfillment is surrender. Surrender embraces the creative flow of the Pattern. Embrace Spirit within yourself. Be willing to release yourself to the Creator's Light. Beginning, ending, and beginning again is your birthright. As the new Human Consciousness unfolds within you, within the Pattern that guides you, release yourself to the creative impulse that came with you into this life.

Be well, be free in Spirit.

# ACKNOWLEDGMENTS

The author wishes to thank the following people:

### ERIN
Grounded in Spirit, always honest, always listened to, sharing a self-ruthlessness worthy of an evolved soul.

### CHRISTINE
A fellow walker in the inner planes of Spirit. An ethical energy healer of vast skills and talents.

### MICHAEL
Backstop to the many experiences that make up the foundation of *The Pattern*, an exploration of hyper-consciousness, readable and authentic.

### KATHERINE JEFFERS
A friend, companion, and enduring presence in my life. I love you.

### DANIEL WEIZMANN
Encouraged me and stood firm on his analysis of this book. Though he would deny it, he helped to shape this complex story into clear and articulate language.

Made in the USA
Middletown, DE
28 September 2022

11374337R00116